REYKJAVÍK

JENNA GOTTLIEB

Contents

Clockwise from top left: colorful house in Reykjavík; downtown Reykjavík; Austurvöllur; Culture Night festival.

DISCOVER

Reykjavík

Reykjavík is having a moment. Relatively affordable airfares are drawing weekenders from both sides of the Atlantic, giving Iceland's capital city a chance to show off its urban appeal and highly individualistic style.

With quaint museums, cool music venues, and top-notch restaurants, small Reykjavík makes a big impression. Stroll the capital's streets and explore the galleries, coffeehouses, intimate concert venues, and music shops—you can't help but feel the city's creative energy. Handcrafted local beers replace specialty coffees as the drink of choice come evening time, when low-key daytime hangouts morph into pulsing parties that fuel Reykjavík's thriving nightlife scene.

Clockwise from top left: pipe organ inside Hallgrímskirkja; Icelandic national costume; northern lights; Reykjavík nightlife; Harpa.

The Best of Reykjavík

Day 1

Explore downtown Reykjavík and all the shops, galleries, restaurants, and coffeehouses the city has to offer. Walk down the street **Skólavörðustígur** to the landmark church **Hallgrímskirkja** to check out the amazing interior, beautiful organ, and view from the top. Grab coffee or lunch on Skólavörðustígur at **Café Babalu,** which makes tasty lattes and light meals like crepes and panini. The street is also where you can pick up a traditional Icelandic sweater at the **Handknitting Association of Iceland.**

Walk down the main street, **Laugavegur,** and pop into the **Hrim** stores for Icelandic design and **Mál og Menning** for books, T-shirts, and other tourist wares. Walk toward city hall and stroll around the man-made pond **Tjörnin,** where you can check out swans, ducks, and other birds.

For dinner, consider one of the city's trendy restaurants, like **Fiskfelagid** for the freshest catch of the day or **Bambus** for Asian fusion. Reykjavík nightlife is epic, and venues like **Húrra** and **Kex Hostel** are perfect for checking out local DJs or live bands and dancing the night away.

Day 2

Reykjavík's harbor has a lot to see. Have breakfast at **Café Haiti** and watch boats enter the harbor. Sign up for a **whale-watching** or **bird-watching** excursion for a chance to spot minke whales, dolphins, fin whales, blue whales, and seabirds (depending on the season). Once back on land, walk to the **Saga Museum** to learn about Iceland's history and enjoy a coffee and snack or light meal at the in-house restaurant, **Matur og Drykkur.** Walk over to **Harpa** concert hall to take in a concert or just check out the amazing interior and architecturally striking exterior.

Walk back downtown and explore the **Reykjavík Art Museum,** then

Reykjavík

Gullfoss waterfall

have dinner at wildly popular sushi restaurant **Osushi**. Stop by **Bar 11** to hear some local live music.

Day 3

Take the day to tour the **Golden Circle**, easily accessible from Reykjavík. It comprises a trio of must-see sights: **Þingvellir National Park,** a geological wonder that is also the birthplace of democracy in Iceland; the geothermal area of **Geysir,** where the hot spring Strokkur erupts every 5-7 minutes; and **Gullfoss,** Iceland's most famous and most photographed waterfall.

Day 4

Go to **Mokka** café on Skólavörðustígur for breakfast—the waffles with homemade jam and fresh cream are delightful. Then visit Reykjavík's best record shops: Head to **12 Tónar,** a few doors up from Mokka, and **Lucky Records** near Hlemmur bus station.

Instead of going directly to the airport, sign up for a bus transfer to the **Blue Lagoon** to enjoy the glorious waters. Then head to Keflavík for your flight.

Reykjavík

Though Reykjavík is small, its energy mimics that of bigger cities like Berlin.

Reykjavík residents are known to have two lives: They work by day, and by night become musicians, artists, novelists, or poets. While strolling on Reykjavík's main street, Laugavegur, you'll see street art among the high-end shops, musicians playing impromptu concerts outside coffeehouses, and small art galleries boasting original "Icelandic Design." It's undeniably a creative city.

Reykjavík's history dates back to AD 874, when Ingólfur Arnarson from Norway established the first settlement in Iceland. The city slowly grew over the centuries, and in 1786, Reykjavík was established as an official trading town. Today, Reykjavík has a lot of people, cars, and trees, in stark contrast to the rest of the country. Roughly 220,000 of Iceland's 340,000 residents live in the capital city.

While Reykjavík can seem quite urban with its galleries and restaurants, nature is never too far away. The air is unbelievably clean, and whales can be seen passing by the harbor during the summer.

PLANNING YOUR TIME

Given its small size, Reykjavík can be "done" in 1-2 days depending on your level of interest. Some travelers treat Reykjavík as their starting point before heading out on the Ring Road or booking day trips into the countryside, while others travel to Reykjavík specifically for the nightlife and art scene.

ORIENTATION

Reykjavík is the most compact capital city in all of Europe. Its downtown and the old harbor are situated in the northern half of the city, and the main bus station (BSÍ) is in the south. Most of the hotels, museums, shops, and restaurants are also in the northern half. The main street in central

Previous: downtown Reykjavík; a park near the Alþingishúsið. **Above:** Hallgrímskirkja.

Look for ★ to find recommended
sights, activities, dining, and lodging.

Highlights

© AVALON TRAVEL

★ **Reykjavík Art Museum (Listasafn Reykjavíkur):** It's three museums in one, showcasing sculpture, contemporary art, and the works of beloved Icelandic artist Jóhannes Kjarval (page 11).

★ **Hallgrímskirkja:** The "Church of Hallgrímur" is a striking national monument dedicated to one of Iceland's most cherished and celebrated poets. Its tower boasts spectacular views (page 15).

★ **National Gallery of Iceland (Listasafn Íslands):** The largest collection of Icelandic art on the island has everything from classic portraits to gorgeous landscapes (page 20).

★ **Tjörnin:** Close to Reykjavík City Hall, this pond is a lovely place to take a stroll and enjoy the birdlife (page 21).

★ **Harpa:** This striking concert hall features individual glass panels that light up during the darkness of winter (page 21).

★ **Sólfar:** The large boat sculpture by the sea has been delighting photographers and tourists for decades (page 22).

★ **Perlan:** This unique dome-shaped building has one of the best views of Reykjavík from its outdoor deck (page 24).

★ **Reykjavík Nightlife:** The capital city may be small, but its nightlife is legendary (page 27).

★ **Hiking Mount Esja:** An easy climb on basalt rock climaxes with gorgeous views out to sea (page 56).

★ **Blue Lagoon (Bláa Lónið):** This gorgeous, geothermally heated spring heals the skin and soothes the body (page 70).

Reykjavík is **Laugavegur,** which starts in the east. As you move west, it eventually becomes Bankastræti, which ends as Austurstræti. The streets tend to have long names, and there isn't a grid system in place, but the city is small enough that you won't get too lost. Hlemmur bus station on the east end of Laugavegur is Strætó's main depot downtown. It can connect you to just about anywhere in central and greater Reykjavík.

Sights

CENTRAL REYKJAVÍK
★ Reykjavík Art Museum
(Listasafn Reykjavíkur)

The **Reykjavík Art Museum** is actually three museums (Hafnarhús, Kjarvalsstaðir, and Ásmundarsafn) in three different locations. Admission is 1,600ISK, and children under 18 and seniors are free. Each museum is open 10am-5pm daily, and if you purchase a ticket to any one of the three museums, you also gain access to the other two—although entry is only available on the same day your ticket was purchased. Each museum is fairly small, and you can hit all three in one day; an hour at each is sufficient.

HAFNARHÚS

Hafnarhús (Tryggvagata 17, tel. 354/590-1200, www.artmuseum.is), which focuses on contemporary art and has three floors of exhibitions, is the crown jewel of the three museums, in part because of its permanent collection of paintings and prints by Erró, one of the most celebrated modern Icelandic artists. His pieces displayed here range from light pop art with bright colors and interesting characters to samples of line sketches from his earlier work. While the art can be playful, Erró also tackles political

Reykjavík's stunning setting

Central Reykjavík

HÓLMASLÓÐ

FARMERS & FRIENDS

FISKISLÓÐ

GRANDAGARÐUR

OLD HARBOR

SEE DETAIL

EIÐSGRANDI

LYF OG HEILSA

ÁNANAUST

GEIRSGATA

HRINGBRAUT

HARPA

GRANDAR

HAFNARHÚS

SEE "DOWNTOWN REYKJAVÍK" MAP

SKÚLAGATA

SÓLFAR

HÖFÐI HUSE

HÓFSVALLAGATA

Hóvallar-garður

SUÐURGATA

CITY HALL

TJÖRNIN

Reykjavík-kurtjörn

LÆKJARGATA

HVERFISGATA

NIGHTLIFE

NATIONAL GALLERY OF ICELAND

BERGSTAÐASTRÆTI

VÍNBERIÐ

FRÍKIRKJUVEGUR

KEX HOSTEL

SÆBRAUT

BORGARTÚN

VESTUR-BÆJARLAUG (POOL)

NEGHAGI

SKOTHÚSVEGUR

HÓTEL HOLT

PÓSGATA

ADAM HOTEL

REYKJAVÍK ROASTERS

KRONKRON

ARGENTINA

FOSSHÓTEL BARON

HVERFISGATA

HLEMMUR SQUARE

BAMBUS

NATIONAL MUSEUM OF ICELAND

Hljómskalagarður

N JARÐGATA

HALLGRÍMS-KIRKJA

BARÓNSSTÍGUR

SUNDHÖLLIN (POOL)

SNORRABRAUT

LUCKY RECORDS

AROUND ICELAND

EINHOLT APARTMENTS

RADISSON BLU SAGA HOTEL/REYKJAVÍK

ÆGISIÐA

UNIVERSITY OF ICELAND

SUÐURGATA

STURLUGATA

NJARÐGATA

SUNNA GUESTHOUSE

EINAR JÓNSSON MUSEUM

EIRÍKSGATA

ROADHOUSE

REYKJAVÍK HOSTEL VILLAGE

ICELAND PHALLOLOGICAL MUSEUM

EINHOLT

STÓRHOLT

FLÓKAGATA

NORDIC HOUSE

Vatnsmýri

HRINGBRAUT

GAMLA HRINGBRAUT

RAUÐARÁRSTÍGUR

KJARVALSSTAÐIR

Klambratún

MIKLABRAUT

LANGAHLÍÐ

NAUTHÓLSVEGUR

FLUGVALLARVEGUR

BÚSTAÐAVEGUR

Valsvöllur

49

REYKJAVÍK DOMESTIC AIRPORT

EINARSNES

ICELANDAIR HOTEL REYKJAVÍK NATURA/ SOLEY NATURA SPA

NAUTHÓLSVEGUR

PERLAN

Öskjuhlíð

© AVALON TRAVEL

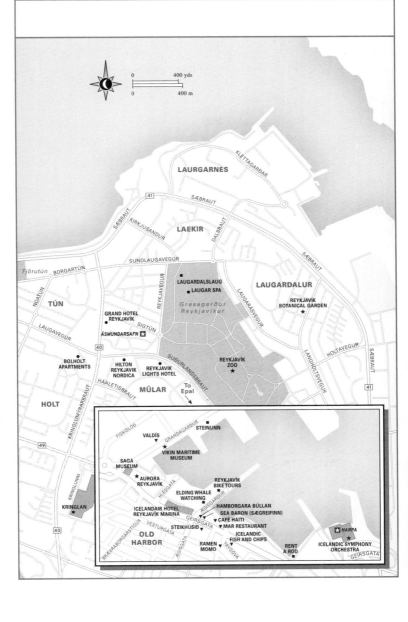

Downtown Reykjavík

Reykjavíkurtjörn

TJÖRNIN

Alþingisgarðurinn

Austurvöllur

Ingólfstorg

Arnarhóll

REYKJAVIK CITY HALL

NATIONAL GALLERY OF ICELAND (LISTASAFN ÍSLANDS)

REYKJAVIK MUSEUM OF PHOTOGRAPHY

HAFNARHÚS

HOTEL REYKJAVIK CENTRUM

FJALAKÖTTURINN

FISH MARKET

KRAUM

HJÓLABÆR

STOFAN CAFÉ

TAPAS BARINN

FISCHERSUND

RESTAURANT REYKJAVIK

HÚRRA

GRILLHÚSIÐ

THE VIKING

NAUSTIN

CENTRUM PLAZA HOTEL

MICRO BAR

THE ENGLISH PUB

RADISSON BLU 1919 HOTEL

BÆJARINS BEZTU PYLSUR (THE TOWN'S BEST HOT DOGS!)

GANDHI RESTAURANT

KOLAPORTIÐ

ALÞINGISHÚSIÐ

IÐNÓ

BERGSSON MATHÚS

KVOSIN HOTEL

EYMUNDSSON

AUSTUR

HÖRNIÐ

OSUSHI

HOTEL BORG

GANLA SMIDJAN PIZZERIA

HRESSO

HRESSINGARSKÁLINN

GRILLMARKET (GRILLMARKAÐURINN)

HÚMARHÚSIÐ

LÆKJARBREKKA

CINTAMANI

AURUM

KAFFITÁR

SUSHI SOCIAL

ICELANDIC OPERA

LOFT HOSTEL

101 HOTEL

DILL RESTAURANT

CULTURE HOUSE ÞJÓÐMENNINGARHÚSIÐ

NATIONAL THEATER OF ICELAND ÞJÓÐLEIKHÚSIÐ

REYKJAVIK4YOU APARTMENTS

ELDUR OG IS

FOA

NIGHTLIFE

66° NORTH

THE VIKING

SUSHIBARINN

MOKKA

ALAFOSS

BAR 11

ÍTALÍA

KAFFIBARINN

GEYSIR

C IS FOR COOKIE

CAFÉ BABALÚ

HANDPRJÓNASAMBAND ÍSLANDS

12 TÓNAR

MAL OG MENNING

ROOM WITH A VIEW

BLUE LAGOON/RAVENS

GLÓ

LEBOWSKI BAR

HOTEL KLÖPP

KIKI QUEER BAR

CAFÉ ROSENBERG

HOTEL FRON

BOSTON

HRÍM

DILLON

HRÍM ELDHÚS

SMEKKLEYSA (BAD TASTE) RECORDS

KRUA THAI

GARDASTRÆTI · TUNGATA · BARUGATA · OLDUGATA · RANARGATA · SUDURGATA · TJARNARGATA · MJOSSTRÆTI · VONARSTRÆTI · KIRKJUSTRÆTI · AÐALSTRÆTI · VALLARSTRÆTI · AUSTURSTRÆTI · HAFNARSTRÆTI · TRYGGVAGATA · GEIRSGATA · TEMPLARASUND · KIRKJUTORG · SKÓLABRÚ · PÓSTHÚSSTRÆTI · FRIKIRKJUVEGUR · LÆKJARGATA · LÆKJARTORG · LAUFÁSVEGUR · BÓKHLÖÐUSTÍGUR · AMTMANNSSTÍGUR · SKÓLASTRÆTI · MIDSTRÆTI · ÞINGHOLTSSTRÆTI · INGÓLFSSTRÆTI · BANKASTRÆTI · SPÍTALASTÍGUR · BERGSTADASTRÆTI · LAUGAVEGUR · HVERFISGATA · LINDARGATA · SKÚLAGATA · SÓLVALLAGATA · SKÓLAVÖRÐUSTÍGUR · VEGAMÓTASTÍGUR · SMIÐJUSTÍGUR · TÝSGATA · NJÁLSGATA · KLAPPARSTÍGUR · GRETTISGATA

0   300 yds
0   300 m

© AVALON TRAVEL

and social issues. Hafnarhús also houses works by other Icelandic artists, as well as rotating exhibitions of foreign painters, designers, and visual artists.

KJARVALSSTAÐIR
Kjarvalsstaðir (Flókagata 24, tel. 354/517-1290, www.artmuseum.is) explores the works of Icelandic painter Jóhannes Kjarval (1885-1972), best known for his dark and moody paintings of Iceland's landscapes. Kjarval was a master of capturing the country's raw nature in the winter light. The majority of Kjarval's collection was left to the city of Reykjavík after his death. The other wing of the museum features various Icelandic artists, ranging from well-known modern artists to some of the country's best and brightest art students. The museum is one level with a coffeehouse in the middle of the two wings, and the high ceilings and wall of windows here creates an interesting space. A large field behind the museum sometimes serves as a spot for sculpture exhibitions.

ÁSMUNDARSAFN
Ásmundarsafn (Sigtún, tel. 354/553-2155, www.artmuseum.is) is an impressive sculpture museum exclusively featuring the works of Ásmundur Sveinsson (1893-1982), who worked with materials including wood, copper, and iron. Ásmundur's work is housed in a gorgeous stark-white domed building. An exhibit features what his workshop looked like and contains renderings of projects, as well as his masterpiece, a chair carved out of wood; the level of detail in the craftsmanship of the chair is spectacular. An outdoor sculpture garden features interesting works of human forms among trees, shrubs, and flowers.

Culture House
(Safnahúsið)
Culture House (Hverfisgata 15, tel. 354/545-1400, www.culturehouse.is, 10am-5pm daily, 2,000ISK) is a stately white neoclassical building that opened as a museum in 1909. It is home to significant medieval manuscripts, including unique sagas, narratives, and poems from early settlers. Guided tours of exhibitions on Mondays and Fridays at 3pm last about an hour, or you can tour on your own. Rotating exhibitions throughout the year can include paintings, photography, or literary works. The exhibits do an excellent job of placing the manuscripts, literature, and artwork in context, giving visitors a great overview. Be sure to check the website to see what's on view. Culture House also plays host to conferences, gatherings, and readings throughout the year, including Reykjavík's annual design festival, DesignMarch, in the spring. The cafeteria serves light meals, and the traditional meat soup is delicious.

★ Hallgrímskirkja
Hallgrímskirkja (Hallgrímstorg, tel. 354/510-1000, www.hallgrimskirkja. is, 9am-9pm daily May 1-Sept. 30, 9am-5pm daily Oct 1-Apr. 30, free) is one

of the most photographed, and most visited, sites in Reykjavík. The "Church of Hallgrímur" is a national monument dedicated to Hallgrímur Pétursson (1614-1674), a poet cherished and celebrated by Icelanders. Hallgrímur is best known for 50 hymns that he wrote, *Hymns of the Passion,* about the passion of Christ. These hymns are familiar to all Icelanders, and are read annually on Icelandic radio before Easter.

The church is a modern structure, made out of concrete, with basalt-style columns at the bottom coming to a point at the top. Standing 73 meters, the Lutheran church was designed by state architect Guðjón Samúelsson. Work started on the building in 1945, and was completed in 1986. Hallgrímskirkja, still an active church that holds services, is a must-see for tourists. The interior is home to a gorgeous organ constructed by Johannes Klais Organworks in Germany, as well as beautiful stained glass windows. Concerts ranging from choirs to organ performances are frequently held; be sure to check the website for upcoming concerts. An annual Christmas concert features traditional songs sung in English.

The highlight of a trip to Hallgrímskirkja for many is a visit to the top of the **tower** (9am-9pm daily May 1-Sept. 30, 9am-5pm daily Oct.1-Apr. 30, 900ISK), which has spectacular views of the city. An elevator takes you up.

Einar Jónsson Museum

The **Einar Jónsson Museum** (Eiríksgata 3, tel. 354/561-3797, www.lej.is, 10am-5pm daily, 1,000ISK, free for children under 18) houses the works of one of Iceland's most celebrated sculptors, Einar Jónsson (1874-1954). Situated across the street from Hallgrímskirkja, the museum features work ranging from Christian-themed sculptures to those depicting Iceland's rich folklore. Einar worked almost entirely with plaster, which was rare for the period. The outdoor sculpture garden is beautiful, whether the sun is shining or if it is under a layer of snow. The garden makes the museum a very

Hallgrímskirkja

Reykjavík is a small, walkable city with a lot to see. While spending at least one day in Reykjavík is recommended, you can see quite a bit in just an hour, which is approximately how long this walk takes without stops. It's ideal to complete this five-kilometer walking tour in the early afternoon, but monitor the weather and decide when it's best for you to go.

- Start your leisurely self-guided walking tour at **Hallgrímskirkja,** where you can explore the interior and head to the top of the tower for a fantastic view over the city.

- Then walk down Skólavörðustígur, the street directly across from the church entrance, to check out some quirky shops and cafés. **Café Babalu** is a nice stop on Skólavörðustígur for a cup of coffee and slice of dynamite carrot cake.

- Continue walking down Skólavörðustígur until you hit **Laugavegur,** the city's main drag and center of life in downtown Reykjavík, and turn left.

- Proceed until you meet Lækjargata street, where you'll turn left and head to **Tjörnin,** a pretty pond where you can watch ducks and swans.

- Walk clockwise around the perimeter on a pondside path, and loop past **Reykjavík City Hall** at the pond's northwest corner.

- Follow Tjarnargata street from here for one block, turning right on Kirkjustræti to see Iceland's Parliament House, **Alþingishúsið,** near Austurvöllur square.

- Then it's time to head toward the harbor; backtrack slightly the way you came, heading west down Kirkjustræti, and turn right onto Aðalstræti, continuing on it as it becomes Vesturgata. Turn right on Mjóstræti and left onto Tryggvagata, crossing the road here and heading east on Geirsgata. In about 400 meters you'll link up with the Sculpture & Shore Walk, a waterfront path that leads to **Harpa** concert hall, a striking architectural gem.

- After some time exploring the building or taking pictures, head 600 meters further southeast along the waterfront walkway to see *Sólfar,* a popular sculpture and another excellent photo opportunity.

- Next, cross Sæbraut at the pedestrian crossing east of the sculpture and turn left onto Skúlagata, continuing about 150 meters until you see **Kex Hostel** on the right; stop for a coffee, beer, snack, or chance to chat with locals and other tourists at this hip and wildly popular spot's bar and lounge area.

- Afterward, exit the hostel to the left and head south on Vitastígur for a couple of blocks, turning right back onto Laugavegur to check out more shops like **Smekkleysa (Bad Taste) Records** or **Mál og Menning** bookshop. You're back in the center of town and will soon connect with the portion of Laugavegur covered earlier in the walk.

special visit. Plan to spend about an hour checking out the art inside, and if the weather is nice, spend additional time outside in the garden.

Icelandic Phallological Museum
(Hið Íslenzka Reðasafn)

The **Icelandic Phallological Museum** (Laugavegur 116, tel. 354/561-6663, www.phallus.is, 10am-6pm daily, 1,500ISK) is just as weird as it sounds. Guests can view the penises of 200 animals, including the arctic fox, walrus, seal, and polar bear. After the museum was moved to its current location in Reykjavík (from Húsavík in North Iceland), the curator unveiled his latest acquisition—a human member. The museum has members on display in glass cases, and preserved bones of certain mammals are hanging on the wall. The highlight is also a unique photo op: the huge whale specimen on display. Some people find the museum humorous, while others are a bit freaked out. Looking for unique postcards, T-shirts, and souvenirs? Look no further.

National Museum of Iceland
(Þjóðminjasafn Íslands)

The **National Museum of Iceland** (Suðurgata 41, tel. 354/530-2200, www.nationalmuseum.is, 10am-5pm daily, 2,000ISK) is Reykjavík's main heritage and history museum, housing everything from tools and clothing of the settlement era to models of Viking-era ships. This is the best museum in the city to get insight on the history of the Icelandic nation and its people. The artifacts and exhibitions are well presented with clear information in English. Budget about two hours to take in all the exhibits.

Saga Museum

The **Saga Museum** (Grandagardi 2, tel. 354/511-1517, www.sagamuseum.is, 10am-6pm daily, 2,100ISK) has 17 exhibits covering everything from

the Saga Museum's restaurant

Iceland's first inhabitants to the nation's conversion to Christianity to the Reformation. Special emphasis is placed on important characters in Iceland's history, such as Ingólfur Arnarson, who is believed to have been Iceland's first settler. There are interactive displays as well as artifacts on view and even a Viking dress-up area that is great for kids; they can play with replicas of traditional clothing and plastic swords. An audio guide in English, German, French, or Swedish is available to accompany your walk around the museum. The in-house restaurant, **Matur og Drykkur,** serves traditional Icelandic food with a modern twist. Budget two hours for this museum.

Nordic House
(Norræna Húsið)

Nordic House (Sturlugata 5, tel. 354/551-7030, www.nordichouse.is, 9am-5pm Sun.-Tue., 9am-9:30pm Wed.-Sat., free) is home to a library, café, and numerous cultural events during the year. Literary and film festivals are held at the building, as well as fashion and music events. Most tourists visit Nordic House for the structure itself. The building, which was opened in 1968, was designed by noted Finnish architect Alvar Aalto, and several of his signature traits are reflected in the design, including the use of tile, white, and wood throughout the building. The one-story building's exterior features a blue ceramic roof.

Reykjavík Museum of Photography
(Ljósmyndasafn Reykjavíkur)

The **Reykjavík Museum of Photography** (Tryggvagata 15, tel. 354/563-1790, www.photomuseum.is, 10am-6pm Mon.-Thurs., 11am-6pm Fri., 1pm-5pm Sat.-Sun., 1,000ISK) has an extensive collection of photographs, as well as items and documents related to the practice of photography, from professional and amateur photographers in Iceland. The collection is

the National Gallery of Iceland

divided into three categories: landscape, press, and portrait photography. The museum is small, but there are a lot of treasures to be found, including the oldest photo in the museum's collection, a landscape photo dating from 1870. Iceland's most famous landscape photographer, Ragnar Axelsson, regularly has photos on exhibit.

★ National Gallery of Iceland
(Listasafn Íslands)

If you have time for only one art museum, make it the **National Gallery of Iceland** (Fríkirkjuvergur 7, tel. 354/515-9600, www.listasafn.is, 10am-5pm daily, 1,500ISK). The National Gallery has a large and varied collection, and houses the country's main collection of Icelandic art. It places particular emphasis on 19th- and 20th-century Icelandic and international art. Here you will see everything from traditional landscape paintings to art depicting the sagas to works by modern Icelandic artists. Works from international artists on display include some from Pablo Picasso and Richard Serra. The stately white building is a stone's throw from Tjörnin (the Pond), so if the weather is fair, taking a leisurely stroll after visiting the museum is quite nice.

Reykjavík City Hall
(Ráðhús Reykjavíkur)

Reykjavík City Hall (Tjarnagata 11, tel. 354/411-1111, www.visitreykjavik. is) is more than just a building that houses the mayor and other officials. Built in 1992, the large white structure has a wall of windows overlooking the Pond. On the ground floor, visitors will find an information desk with maps and tourist brochures, as well as a cozy café with a great view of the Pond and city. A large hall is often used for art exhibitions and markets, and a huge model of Iceland is a favorite among tourists and worth a visit.

Reykjavík harbor

★ Tjörnin

Tjörnin (the Pond) is a small body of water, rich with birdlife, situated next to Reykjavík City Hall. The scenic strip of colorful houses surrounding the Pond begs to be photographed. When the weather is nice, a walk around the Pond, which is about 1.5 kilometers around, is delightful. Sculptures and benches dot the perimeter. Birdlife is plentiful, with arctic terns, ducks, gulls, and swans. Feeding the birds is not allowed, so don't be that tourist who empties a bag of stale bread at the edge. In the winter, the water freezes and it becomes a popular spot for ice-skating.

Alþingishúsið

Alþingishúsið, or Parliament House, is the meeting place of the national parliament members of Iceland. Iceland's democracy dates back to the year 930, when parliament members met at Þingvellir; the parliament was moved to Reykjavík in 1844. Situated near Austurvöllur park, the stone building was designed by Danish architect Ferdinand Meldahland and built in 1881. Currently, only the debating chamber and a few small meeting rooms are actually located in the building. Offices of most of Alþingi's members are in other buildings in the area around Austurvöllur, which is actually the address of the building. It's not possible to attend sessions of parliament.

OLD HARBOR

Reykjavík's old harbor has been undergoing a transformation over the past few years, and it's become a dynamic place to visit, with shops, museums, new hotels, and the Ólafur Elíasson-designed Harpa concert hall.

★ Harpa

Harpa (Austurbakki 2, tel. 354/528-5000, www.harpa.is) is a striking glass structure that hosts rock concerts, operas, the Icelandic Symphony, and

Harpa

international conferences. Designed by Icelandic-Danish artist Ólafur Elíasson, the concert hall's exterior features individual glass panels that light up during the darkness of winter, sometimes blinking in a pattern or simply changing colors, and the building's waterside location lends itself to lovely reflections. Since opening its doors in 2011, Harpa has been lauded by design organizations and magazines around the world. Daily 30-minute guided tours of the building are available (1,500ISK, year-round) eight times a day mid-June-August and three times a day from the end of August to mid-June. It's also just a fun place to explore and take pictures of, even if you're not going to attend a concert or conference. **Smurstöðin** (10am-6pm daily), a café on the bottom floor, serves coffee, soft drinks, light meals, and cakes, and **Kolabrautin** (4pm-11pm daily), a formal restaurant on the 4th floor, has stunning views of the harbor.

Höfði House

Höfði House (Borgartún) is one of Reykjavík's most historically significant buildings and worth a photo or two. Built in 1909, the stately white building was initially used as the French consulate, and later served as a sort of guesthouse for famous folks passing through including Winston Churchill, Queen Elizabeth II, and even actress Marlene Dietrich. Perhaps its most famous use was as the backdrop for a 1986 meeting between U.S. president Ronald Reagan and the head of the Soviet Union, Mikhail Gorbachev. Today, Höfði is owned by the city of Reykjavík and is used for official receptions and meetings. Although the house is not open to the public, visitors are welcome to explore the exterior of the building.

★ Sólfar

Situated near a coastal path popular with cyclists and runners, *Sólfar* (by Sæbraut street) is a huge stainless steel sculpture described as a dreamboat. Before Harpa was built, *Sólfar* was the top spot to take photos near

Sólfar, the *Sun Voyager*, by sculptor Jón Gunnar Árnason

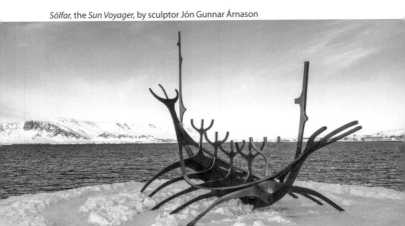

the harbor. It remains a big draw for tourists and is definitely worth a visit. **23**
Icelandic sculptor Jón Gunnar Árnason (1931-1989) wanted to convey a
sense of undiscovered territory, hope, progress, and freedom, and built
the piece as an ode to the sun, hence the name, translated as *Sun Voyager*.
The sculpture was unveiled in 1990, just months after the artist's death.
The view of Mount Esja, the sea, and passing boats is the perfect backdrop
for photos. On clear days, you can see the town of Akranes across the bay.

Aurora Reykjavík

Aurora Reykjavík (Grandagarður 2, tel. 354/780-4500, www.aurorareykja-
vik.is, 9am-9pm daily, 1,600ISK) gives you a chance to check out northern
lights in any season. If you can't make it to Iceland in the wintertime, this
is the next best thing. The multimedia exhibition gives a history of the aurora borealis, relates stories of northern lights from around the world, and
provides an introduction to northern lights photography. The highlight of
the center is a 13-minute film that shows some of the most majestic northern lights displays over the island.

Vikin Maritime Museum

Vikin Maritime Museum (Grandargarður 8, tel. 354/517-9400, www.bor-
garsgusafn.is, 10am-5pm daily, 1,600ISK) is Reykjavík's main museum
devoted to the city's fishing history. The exhibitions show the progression
from rowboats to modern trawlers and describe the vessels used, trading
routes, and the construction of Reykjavík's harbor. There are daily tours
of the coastal vessel *Odinn* available at 11am, 1pm, 2pm, and 3pm that
last about an hour. The exhibitions cover the city's fishing history from
the settlement to the present day. The museum café has great views of the
harbor and offers an outdoor eating area when the weather cooperates.

OUTSIDE THE CITY CENTER
Reykjavík Zoo
(Fjölskyldu- og Húsdýragarðinum)

The **Reykjavík Zoo** (Laugardalur, tel. 354/575-7800, www.mu.is, 10am-
6pm daily June-late Aug., 10am-5pm daily late Aug.-May, 860ISK adults
and teenagers, 650ISK children 5-12, free for children 4 and under) is more
park than zoo. You won't see monkeys or polar bears, but exhibits house
horses, pigs, goats, sheep, and other farm animals. The main attraction
is a pair of seals. It's a pleasant place to walk around and bring children,
but it isn't much of a tourist destination; if you're not on a long trip with
small children, you can skip the zoo and not feel bad about it. Inside is a
tiny aquarium that houses mainly fish. In the summer months, you'll see
Icelandic families taking a stroll, looking at the animals, and visiting a
small play area for children. There isn't an official petting zoo, but it's common to see parents holding their children up to pet horses in a penned area.

Reykjavík Botanical Garden
(Grasagardur Reykjavíkur)

The **Reykjavík Botanical Garden** (Laugardalur, tel. 354/411-8650, www. grasagardur.is, 10am-10pm daily May 1-Sept. 30, 10am-3pm daily Oct. 1-Apr. 30, free) is a beautiful spot tucked away in a quiet part of the city. East of downtown Reykjavík, the neighborhood is more residential. During the summer months, the garden is chock-full of bright flowers, hardy plants, peaceful ponds, and thriving birdlife. The café within the garden, Café Flora, is a little-known spot among tourists. You will find locals sipping on coffee drinks and enjoying light meals while taking in the view from grand windows. If you're not visiting in the summer, you can skip the garden.

★ Perlan

Perlan (Öskjuhlíð, tel. 354/562-0200, www.perlanmuseum.is), nicknamed "the Pearl," is the distinctive, dome-shaped structure in Reykjavík's skyline. It offers one of the best views of the city skyline from its outdoor viewing platform (10am-10pm daily, 490ISK)—you can walk the perimeter and get a perfect panorama. The interior underwent a significant renovation in 2017, and the public building now hosts exhibits (2,900ISK), kicked off by an installation on glaciers and ice caves. A planetarium and northern lights exhibition are planned for fall 2018. Perlan also has a café that serves coffee and light meals as well as a souvenir shop.

Sports and Recreation

WHALE-WATCHING

Whale-watching is in some ways the best part of natural Reykjavík, in that you get to see a slice of nature just minutes from shore. **Elding Whale Watching** (Ægisgarður 5, tel. 354/519-5000, www.elding.is), which has 12 boats in Reykjavík, offers tours year-round and boasts a 95 percent chance of seeing whales in the summer, and 80 percent chance in the winter. Guides are enthusiastic, and the business is one of the oldest at the harbor. Tourists relish the sightings of minke and humpback whales, dolphins, porpoises, and various seabirds, including puffins and arctic terns. Make sure you dress warmly, even in the summer, as it can get quite cold on the open waters. Tours are about three hours and cost 10,990ISK for adults and 5,495ISK for children 7-15, free for children 6 and under. **Special Tours** (Ægisgarður 13, tel. 354/560-8800, www.specialtours.is) has a fleet of five boats of different speeds and sizes and also runs year-round tours from Reykjavík harbor, with five daily departures May-August and 1-2 daily departures the remainder of the year. Tours are about three hours and cost 10,990ISK per person. Both companies have environmentally responsible whale-watching policies.

BIKING

Reykjavík is a wonderful city to see by bicycle—that is, when the weather holds up. Over the past few years, there has been an initiative to designate more bike lanes and establish more places to lock up your bicycle along the streets. This isn't Amsterdam, but Reykjavík has come a long way. If you're in town and would like to rent a bike for an independent ride, or join a tour, **Reykjavík Bike Tours** (Ægisgarður 7, tel. 354/694-8956, www.icelandbike.com) will get you going. Its "Classic Reykjavík Bike Tour" (7,500ISK) covers about seven kilometers and takes a good 2.5 hours. Along the tour, you will see the University of Iceland campus, Reykjavík's Catholic cathedral, the parliament house, the old harbor, and more. Bicycle rentals start at 3,500ISK for four hours.

BIRD-WATCHING

For bird-watchers, the "Puffin Express" tour, which leaves from Reykjavík harbor May through mid-August, is operated by **Special Tours** (tel. 354/560-8800, www.specialtours.is). The owners have been running bird-watching tours since 1996, provide binoculars on board, and have a 100 percent sighting success rate. The guides have a soft spot for the funny black and white birds with the brilliant beaks and take great pride in telling you all about them. A one-hour boat tour is 5,700ISK for adults and 2,850ISK for children.

FISHING

If you'd like to try your hand at reeling in one of Iceland's freshest fish during the summer, you can rent equipment at Reykjavík harbor from **Rent a Rod** (tel. 354/869-2840, www.rentarod.is, 10am-6pm Mon.-Fri., 11am-5pm Sat.-Sun. June-Aug.). For 2,990ISK, you can rent a rod with reel and line for two hours, including bait, single-use gloves, and map of the harbor. You can catch trout, salmon, cod, pollock, and haddock. The staff could also arrange for fishing day tours out of the harbor. For sea angling tours, check out **Elding Whale Watching** (Ægisgarður 5, tel. 354/519-5000, www.elding.is), which offers a tour with a "gourmet" twist, where you can cook and eat your catch on board the boat. The tour is available May-August. The tour is about three hours, departs daily from Reykjavík harbor at 11am, and costs 17,800ISK.

SWIMMING

Swimming is a central part of Icelandic culture, and if you don't visit a pool or two during your stay in Iceland, you're missing out. Icelanders treat the pools as places for social gatherings. Visitors will see groups of friends and/or family in the pools and relaxing in hot tubs, chatting, laughing, and catching up. Each pool has its own character and local flavor, and some pools are more child-friendly than others, with slides and bigger areas designated for children. And, for roughly $5, it's a great way to spend a few leisurely hours. The pools listed here are recommended.

Laugardalslaug (Sundlaugavegur 30, tel. 354/411-5100, 7am-10pm Mon.-Fri., 8am-8pm Sat.-Sun., 950ISK) is the biggest pool facility in Reykjavík, and the one that gets the most tourists. The heated 50-meter outdoor pool is a big draw, along with the hot tubs, steam bath, and sauna. It's very crowded in the summer months (June-August) and can be loud because the giant waterslide in the children's pool is a favorite among local kids.

Sundhöllin (Barónstígur, tel. 354/551-4059, 7am-10pm Mon.-Fri., 8am-7pm Sat.-Sun., 950ISK) is the only indoor pool in Reykjavík and popular among locals and tourists alike. The outdoor sundeck overlooking Hallgrímskirkja is a great spot to spend a couple of hours when the sun is shining. Sundhöllin also has a steam room and two hot tubs. Given its proximity to the city center, the pool gets a lot of traffic.

Vesturbæjarlaug (Hofsvallagata 104, tel. 354/566-6879, 7am-10pm Mon.-Fri., 8am-10pm Sat.-Sun., 950ISK) is situated in a quiet neighborhood west of the city center. If you're looking to beat the crowds and experience the pool culture among locals, this is the spot. Facilities include a 25-meter pool, a few hot tubs, and a sauna.

SPAS

If you're after something more luxurious than a local swimming pool, there are a couple of spas in Reykjavík where you can relax and get treatments. Many tourists opt to spend an afternoon at the Blue Lagoon near Grindavík, and several buses depart from the bus station BSÍ (www.bsi.is). But if you want to beat the crowds, a local spa is a great option.

Laugar Spa (Sundlaugavegur 30A, tel. 354/553-0000, www.worldclass. is, 6am-11pm Mon.-Fri., 8am-9:30pm Sat., 8am-7:30pm Sun.) is Reykjavík's largest private spa, offering an extensive menu of treatments including facials, body massage and scrub, tanning treatments, waxing and nail services, and clay wrap treatments. The spa is marketed as an "aquatic heaven," and it's as good as it sounds. The entrance to the spa is reminiscent of a cave, with the soothing sound of water drops falling from a six-meter-wide waterfall. Inside, six sauna rooms are kept at different temperatures, each with its own unique theme. The treatment rooms feature muted hues and calming music. There is an on-site gym, as well as a café serving fresh, healthy meals.

Icelandair Hótel Reykjavík Natura's **Soley Natura Spa** (Nautholsvegur 2, tel. 354/444-4085, www.icelandairhotels.com, 10am-8pm Mon.-Fri., 10am-7pm Sat., noon-5pm Sun.) has an earthy atmosphere with natural hues and lots of wood furnishings. It's Scandinavian to a T. Guests have access to a heated pool, hot tub, and sauna before and after treatments. Massage options include lymphatic massage, hot stone massage, reflexology, and pregnancy massage. Beauty treatments include waxing services, manicures and pedicures, and facials. Access is 3,000ISK for hotel guests, 4,900ISK for nonguests. The spa is only open to guests 16 years of age and older.

Entertainment and Events

★ NIGHTLIFE

Reykjavík may be small, but its nightlife is epic. Whether you're up for some live music, want to dance, or are interested a classic pub crawl, Reykjavík will not disappoint. The main drag, Laugavegur, is ground zero for the hottest clubs and bars in town. If you are up for dancing, Kiki Queer Bar is your spot. If you fancy a whiskey bar, Dillon is the place. If you want to catch a hot Reykjavík band performing live, Húrra is your best bet. Be prepared for it to be a late night and for your wallet to take a hit. Locals don't venture out until around midnight, and drinks are expensive. Expect to pay upwards of 1,000ISK for a pint of beer and 2,200ISK for a cocktail; for this reason, cocktail bars are scarce, and beer is the favored beverage. But, for such a small city, you can't help but be impressed by the number of hot spots catering to different genres. Your biggest challenge will be narrowing down your options!

Bars

Austur (Austurstræti 7, tel. 354/568-1907, 8pm-1am Wed-Thurs., 8pm-4:30am Fri.-Sat.) was once the hottest club in Reykjavík, but a dress code and competition from other clubs have knocked it down a couple of pegs. It's still a place to mingle with locals and dance the night away to trendy dance music.

Boston (Laugavegur 28B, tel. 354/577-3200, 2pm-1am Sun.-Thurs., 2pm-3am Fri.-Sat.) is best known as a hangout for local artists, writers, hipsters, and hangers-on. The bar has an unassuming exterior, but inside await good drinks and hot music, mainly rock. If there's a concert on the night you go, expect to stand shoulder to shoulder. It's a tight spot and doesn't take too long to draw a big crowd.

Hressingarskálinn (Austurstræti 22, tel. 354/561-2240, www.hresso.is, 9am-1am Sun.-Thurs., 10am-4:30am Fri.-Sat.), simply known as Hresso, is a casual restaurant by day, serving up hamburgers and sandwiches. Free Wi-Fi attracts writers, tourists, and locals, who are known to spend hours sipping endless cups of coffee. By night, Hresso transforms into a dance club, with hot DJs and live bands. Expect trendy dance music.

Lebowski Bar (Laugavegur 20, tel. 354/552-2300, www.lebowski.is, 11:30am-1am Sun.-Thurs., 11:30am-4am Fri.-Sat.) pays not-so-subtle homage to the Coen brothers movie *The Big Lebowski*. Inside there is bowling paraphernalia, posters from the film, and even a rug hanging on the side of the bar. It's a casual eatery during the day, like many of Reykjavík's bars, but at night it transforms into a pretty wild scene, playing the latest dance music. There's a dance floor in the back of the room. The cost of a White Russian, the cocktail famously featured in the film, costs 1,700ISK.

The English Pub (Austurstræti 12b, tel. 354/578-0400, www.enskibar-inn.is, noon-1am Mon.-Fri., noon-4:30am Sat.-Sun.) is part English pub,

Lebowski Bar

Kiki Queer Bar

part sports bar. There's a nice selection of Icelandic and foreign beer, and Guinness is on tap. If there's a soccer game being played anywhere in the world, it will likely be shown on one of the many screens in the bar. If there's a Premier League game on, expect a crowd of expats, tourists, and locals.

Kaffibarinn (Bergstaðastræti 1, tel. 354/551-1588, 5pm-1am Sun.-Thurs., 3pm-3am Fri.-Sat.) has been a Reykjavík institution since scenes from the indie film *101 Reykjavík* were filmed here. Damon Albarn, the Blur front man, used to own a stake in the bar. It's a tiny space, with a rich red exterior that gets jam-packed during the weekends, but it's one of those places that it's cool to say you were there. Expect trendy dance music to be blaring as you enter.

Micro Bar (Austurstræti 6, tel. 354/847-9084, 4pm-midnight daily) is a beer lover's paradise. The bar carries about 80 different beers from countries including Belgium, Germany, Denmark, and the United States. The big draws are the wide selection of Icelandic beers on tap and the number of Icelandic craft beers available. Stop by and try a local stout, pale ale, or lager. The atmosphere is relaxed and relatively quiet, with dim lighting and a large wood bar. You'll find locals at the tables enjoying a beer and conversation with friends.

Gay and Lesbian

Kiki Queer Bar (Laugavegur 22, tel. 354/571-0194, www.kiki.is, 8pm-1am Thurs., 8pm-4:30am Fri.-Sat.) is Reykjavík's only gay bar and was a welcome addition to the scene. Many locals will tell you this is *the* place to go to dance because it attracts some of the best local and visiting DJs. You can expect music ranging from Lady Gaga to the latest Icelandic pop music.

Live Music

Bar 11 (Hverfisgata 18, tel. 354/690-6021, noon-1am Sun.-Thurs., noon-3am Fri.-Sat.) has earned its reputation as Reykjavík's leading rock bar by featuring a steady stream of up-and-coming rock bands as well as local favorites. The decor is dark, with skulls and black furnishings, but the attitude is light and fun.

Café Rósenberg (Lækjargata 2, tel. 354/551-8008, 11am-1am Sun.-Thurs., 11am-3am Fri.-Sat.) hosts jazz, pop, rock, and folk acts from all around Iceland. You have a good chance to catch local favorites like KK, Ellen, and Svavar Knutur here, as well as international acts. The staffers are warm and friendly music lovers who take pride in booking varied acts and running a laid-back café that serves classic Icelandic comfort food.

Dillon (Laugavegur 30, tel. 354/511-2400, 2pm-1am Sun.-Thurs., 2pm-3am Fri.-Sat.) looks and feels like a dive bar. Rockers, metalheads, and hipsters unite, listening to live bands and sipping from the fine collection of more than 150 whiskeys available. Guests can find Scotch and bourbon as well as small-batch Icelandic whiskeys. When there isn't live music, locals DJs keep the music flowing. The interior is a little rough, with lots of wood and not many places to sit, and the music is always loud.

Húrra (Tryggvagata 22, tel. 354/691-9662, 5pm-1am Sun.-Thurs., 5pm-4:30am Fri.-Sat.) is a colorful spot featuring a steady stream of Iceland's hottest bands taking the stage, playing everything from rock and dance to pop and hip-hop, depending on the night.

Kex Hostel (Skúlagata 28, tel. 354/561-6060, www.kexhostel.is) has become a Reykjavík institution over the past few years. The building, formerly a biscuit factory, is a great space, complete with mid-century furniture, vintage wall maps, and a lot of curiosities. A small stage in the entryway hosts up-and-coming bands while guests drink and hang out at the **bar** (11:30am-11pm daily). A back room serves as a venue for more formal concerts. If you're in your 20s and aren't bothered by hipsters, this is your place. Since this is a hostel, it's open 24 hours, so check listings at www.grapevine. is for concert times.

Loft Hostel (Bankastræti 7, tel. 354/553-8140, www.lofthostel.is) has earned a reputation as a place to see and be seen. The 4th-floor bar/café hosts up-and-coming bands, established live acts, and DJs. An outdoor deck overlooks Bankastræti and is packed with locals and tourists alike when the sun is shining during the day, and filled with mingling concertgoers at night. Since this is a hostel, it's open 24 hours, so check listings at www. grapevine.is for concert and event times.

PERFORMING ARTS
Icelandic Opera
(Íslenska Óperan)

The **Icelandic Opera** (Ingólfsstræti 2A, tel. 354/511-6400, www.opera.is) has been thriving since productions moved in 2011 to the exquisite Harpa concert hall by the harbor. Productions have become more elaborate, and entire runs have been selling out. If you are an opera fan, check the website to see the current and upcoming shows. Past performances include *Carmen, Il Trovatore, La Boheme,* and *The Magic Flute.*

Icelandic Symphony Orchestra
(Sinfóníuhljómsveit Íslands)

The **Icelandic Symphony Orchestra** (Austurbakki 2, tel. 354/545-2500, www.sinfonia.is) consists of 90 full-time members and performs about 60 concerts each season, including subscription concerts in Reykjavík, family concerts, school concerts, and recordings, as well as local and international tours. Based in the Harpa concert hall, the symphony has performed works by Igor Stravinsky, Sergei Rachmaninoff, and Pyotr Tchaikovsky.

National Theater of Iceland
(Þjóðleikhúsið)

The **National Theater of Iceland** (Hverfisgata 19, tel. 354/551-1200, www.leikhusid.is) has been a Reykjavík mainstay since its opening in 1950. The emphasis is on Nordic/Scandinavian plays and musicals, but some foreign works are translated into Icelandic. In 2017, the theater put on productions of *Othello* and *Peter and the Wolf* in the 500-seat main stage. The exterior is a cold, concrete-gray building, but inside is a different story. The interior is modern, the theater is comfortable, and there's a lovely lounge area with plush seats and small tables where you can have a drink and wait for the show to begin.

FESTIVALS AND EVENTS
Spring

The **Reykjavík Fashion Festival** (www.rff.is) showcases fashion lines from established designers as well as up-and-comers every March for four days. Along with runway shows and special exhibitions, the festival welcomes international designers as guest speakers. The focus in recent years has been on Icelandic designers and Icelandic guest speakers.

Coinciding with the Reykjavík Fashion Festival is **DesignMarch (HönnunarMars)** (www.designmarch.is), a broader event that covers everything from product design to graphic design. With pop-up stores around the city and exhibitions held in museums and open-air spaces, the festival attracts people from around the world to check out the latest and greatest in Icelandic design.

You may not expect Reykjavík to be a blues town, but don't tell that to locals. The **Reykjavík Blues Festival (Blúshátíð í Reykjavík)** (www.blues.is) is a weeklong event held in early April. It mixes local talent with acclaimed international acts like Michael Burks, Lucky Peterson, Pinetop Perkins, and Magic Slim and the Teardrops.

Gamers rejoice! The **EVE Fanfest** takes over the city every May, celebrating the beloved video game *EVE,* which is the creation of local company CCP. Thousands of gamers, nerds, and curious locals gather, attend roundtable discussions, play live tournaments, and indulge in a pub crawl.

Summer

Delighting locals and tourists since 1970, the **Reykjavík Arts Festival** fresh, showcasing visual and performance artists from around the globe. The festival spans two weeks over late May and early June and holds events in different cultural venues as well as outdoor exhibitions.

Reykjavík Pride (Hinsegin Dagar) (www.reykjavikpride.com) is a city-wide celebration of human rights, diversity, and culture. It garners a huge turnout every year. Each August, the city hosts rainbow-themed events ranging from concerts to guest speakers. It's known as the highest-profile event for Iceland's gay, lesbian, bisexual, and transgender community. Hundreds of volunteers organize the event, and people from around the country congregate to celebrate their fellow citizens.

Since 1990, the **Reykjavík Jazz Festival (Jazzhátíð Reykjavíkur)** (www.reykjavikjazz.is) has been delighting horn section enthusiasts. International artists like Aaron Parks and Chris Speed are invited to put on concerts and jam with locals over five days in mid-August. There are off-venue free events throughout the city, and this is a popular festival among the locals. Headline concerts take place at the concert hall Harpa.

Independent choreographers launched the **Reykjavík Dance Festival** (www.reykjavikdancefestival.com) in 2002, and the annual event is still going strong today. The focus is on bringing contemporary dance closer to the people. The weeklong event held every August showcases local talent as well as international dancers.

Reykjavík Culture Night (Menningarnótt) (www.culturenight.is) has the darling slogan "come on in," which is a reference to the island's old-fashioned customs of hospitality. Culture Night actually starts during the day, with select residents opening up their properties to offer waffles and coffee to their neighbors and visitors. Hundreds of events around the city range from cultural performances to free museum events. The festival culminates with a huge outdoor concert that features some of the biggest names in Icelandic rock and pop music. It's held at the end of August.

Fall

Beginning at the end of September, the **Reykjavík International Film Festival** (www.riff.is) takes place over 11 days, during which films from more than 40 countries are screened. They range from short films to full-length features and documentaries, and the festival is a great venue to discover new talent. Invited special guests have included American director Jim Jarmusch and English director Mike Leigh.

Iceland Airwaves (www.icelandairwaves.is) has been delighting music lovers since 1999. The five-day festival, held in late October/early November, has hosted an impressive list of performers, including Sigur Rós, Björk, and Of Monsters and Men, as well as international artists including Robyn, Kraftwerk, and Flaming Lips. There are also off-venue performances held for free in bars, bookstores, record shops, and coffee-houses—so if you don't score tickets to the festival, you can still check out some amazing music. A detailed off-venue schedule is published along with on-venue appearances.

Winter

Sónar Reykjavík (www.sonarreykjavik.com) is the new kid on the block in Reykjavík music festivals. Launched in 2013, Sónar features rock, pop, punk, electronic, and dance music performances in Harpa concert hall. Artists have included GusGus, Squarepusher, and Hermigervill. The festival takes place in mid-February.

The annual **Reykjavík Food & Fun Festival** (www.foodandfun.is) showcases the culinary exploits of world-renowned chefs collaborating with local Icelandic chefs. There are competitions, exhibitions, and lots of eating. It takes place at the end of February.

Shopping

Reykjavík may not strike you as a shopping destination, but there are quite a few local brands, like clothing labels 66 North and Cintamanti, that are quite popular. If you're up for some shopping, be sure to take a stroll on Laugavegur: The street is chock-full of design shops, jewelers, boutiques, and bookstores.

ART/DESIGN

Aurum (Bankstræti 4, tel. 354/551-2770, www.aurum.is, 10am-6pm daily) is the place to go for unique Icelandic jewelry. Shoppers are treated to an impressive display of rings, necklaces, and earrings made from silver, gold, or lava stones. Aurum's jewelry is distinctively Icelandic, with pieces inspired by the raw nature of the island. An adjoining section is dedicated to modern toys, knitwear, accessories, and home goods.

Epal (Laugavegur 70, tel. 354/551-3555, www.epal.is, 10am-8pm Mon.-Sat., noon-8pm Sun.) is the original design store in Iceland, stocking everything from furniture to light fixtures to bedding and small goods. At Epal, which was founded in 1975, you'll find Icelandic designers as well as international brands, including Fritz Hansen, Georg Jensen, Marimekko, OK Design, and Tin Tin. Other than the downtown Reykjavík store, Epal has three other stores at Skeifan, Keflavík International Airport, and Harpa concert hall.

Foa (Laugavegur 2, tel. 354/571-1433, 10am-6pm Mon.-Sat., 1pm-5pm Sun.) carries indie design brands that can't be found in many other stores. For instance, hand-carved wooden swans by local artist Bjarni Þór are on sale along with small woolen goods for kids and individual letterpress cards. It's a fun store to wander around and pick up something unique.

Hrim Hönnunarhús (Laugavegur 25, tel. 354/553-3003, www.hrim.is, 10am-6pm Mon.-Sat., 1pm-5pm Sun.) is where you go for one-stop shopping for design lovers, whether you're looking for accessories, playful paper goods, or housewares. There is an emphasis on Icelandic design, especially when it comes to jewelry and home goods, but there are also foreign-made items as well. For instance, Hrim has an impressive Lomography camera display for those looking for lo-fi film or a new Diana plastic camera. The staff is friendly and eager to help you find that perfect purchase.

Hrim Eldhus (Laugavegur 32, tel. 354/553-2002, 10am-6pm daily) opened in 2014 after the success of parent shop Hrim, down the block. Eldhus, which means "kitchen" in Iceland, focuses on modern design accessories for the kitchen and dining room. The adorable store stocks goods from local Icelandic designers as well as designers from its Scandinavian and Nordic neighbors. This store is stocked with nothing you really need, but everything you want.

Kraum (Laugavegur 18, tel. 354/779-6161, www.kraum.is, 9am-9pm Mon.-Fri., 10am-9pm Sat- Sun.) has been voted "the best place to stock up on local design" by local newspaper *Reykjavík Grapevine* for straight five years. Kraum stocks everything from the adorable independent children's clothing line As We Grow to handbags made from fish leather. They also carry pillows, jewelry, candleholders, and woolen goods. If you're going to visit one design shop in Reykjavík, it should be Kraum, as it has the largest and most diverse selection of goods.

BOOKSTORES

Reykjavík was named a UNESCO City of Literature in 2012, and the title was well deserved. Locals like to boast that 1 in 10 Icelanders will publish a book in their lifetime and that Iceland has the highest number of Nobel Prize winners for literature per capita. That would be one winner—Halldór Laxness for *Independent People*. Due to the importance of literature to the city and the exceptionally high literacy rate of its citizens, Reykjavík boasts an unusually large number of bookstores.

Eymundsson (Austurstræti 18, tel. 354/540-2000, www.eymundsson.is,

Hrim Eldhus

10am-10pm daily) is the oldest and largest bookstore chain in Reykjavík, dating back to 1872. The main shop on Austurstræti has four levels, with an impressive magazine section, tourist books on Iceland, and a large English-language book section.

Mál og Menning (Laugavegur 18, tel. 354/515-2500, www.malogmenning.is, 9am-10pm daily), which means "Language and Culture," is a favorite among Reykjavík locals. The three-level store sells fun tourist wares on the ground floor next to the magazine section. Upstairs is a collection of art and photography books, along with hundreds of English-language novels and nonfiction reads. The top floor also houses a café, where people sip lattes as they flip through magazines and newspapers.

MUSIC

Icelandic music is more than Björk and Sigur Rós, and a few choice music shops will help you discover local favorites as well as up-and-coming Icelandic artists.

A lot more than a record shop, 12 Tónar (Skólavörðustígur 15, tel. 354/511-5656, www.12tonar.is, 10am-6pm Mon.-Sat., noon-6pm Sun.) is a place to mingle with other music lovers and sample new Icelandic music with private CD players and headphones, all while sipping on a complimentary cup of coffee. The shop was founded in 1998 and is an integral part of Reykjavík's music culture; the owner also runs an independent music label, and the shop is often used as a music venue during Reykjavík's annual autumn music festival, Iceland Airwaves. This is a landmark, a cultural institution.

If you like vinyl, Lucky Records (Rauðarárstígur 10, tel. 354/551-1195, www.luckyrecords.is, 10am-6pm Mon.-Fri., 11am-5pm Sat.-Sun.) is the place for you. The shop has the largest collection of new and used vinyl in the city, with an extensive Icelandic selection as well as foreign rock, pop, hip-hop, jazz, soul, and everything else you could imagine. Bands and

coffee at Mál og Menning bookshop

DJs frequently play free concerts at the shop, and it's a fun place to spend a couple of hours. There's a turntable and headphones, with which you're welcome to sample used records.

Smekkleysa (Bad Taste) Records (Laugavegur 28, tel. 354/534-3730, www.smekkleysa.net, 10am-6pm Mon.-Fri., 10am-5pm Sat., noon-5pm Sun.) was born from the legendary Smekkleysa record label that has released albums from the Sugarcubes (Björk's former band), Sigur Rós, and scores of other Icelandic artists. Its record shop, while small, has a great collection of Icelandic music on CD and vinyl, as well as a DVD section, box sets, and classical music on CD.

Reykjavík Record Shop (Klapparstígur 35, tel. 354/561-2299, 11am-6pm Mon.-Fri., 1pm-6pm Sat.) is a small shop specializing in vinyl that has an impressive selection of local music as well as international artists. You can browse new and used records, as well as CDs, books, and T-shirts.

CLOTHING/KNITWEAR

Perhaps Iceland's best-known and oldest brand, **66 North** (Bankastræti 5, tel. 354/535-6600, www.66north.com, 9am-10pm daily) has been keeping Icelanders warm since 1926. You will find hats, rainwear, gloves, fleece, vests, and parkas in colors ranging from basic black (a favorite among Icelanders) to lava orange. Heavy parkas cost an arm and a leg (around $500), but you pay for the Thermolite insulation and design details. If you're not looking to make a fashion investment, you can grab a hat for about $25.

Cintamani (Bankastræti 7, tel. 354/533-3390, www.cintamani.is, 9am-9pm daily) has been dressing Icelanders in colorful, fashionable designs since 1989. Ranging from base layers to outerwear, Cintamani is a bit more playful than 66 North, with more prints and brighter colors. The emphasis is not just on style, but warmth as well with top-notch insulation.

Farmers & Friends (Laugavegur 37, tel. 354/552-1960, www.farmersmarket.is, 10am-10pm Mon.-Fri., 11am-7pm Sat., 11am-5pm Sun) is

12 Tónar music shop

the flagship store of the wildly popular Farmer's Market clothing label. If you are looking for sweaters other than the traditional garb available at Handprjónasamband Íslands (Handknitting Association of Iceland), Farmer's Market offers everything from cardigans to capes in stylish colors and patterns. The label, which was launched in 2005, is focused on combining classic Nordic design elements with a modern aesthetic.

Geysir (Skólavörðustígur 16, tel. 354/519-6000, www.geysir.com, 10am-7pm Mon.-Sat., 11am-5pm Sun.) features clothes that combine beauty with the utility of Icelandic wool. Warm sweaters, cardigans, capes, and blankets are on offer at the flagship Reykjavík shop, not too far from Hallgrímskirkja. The clothes have a traditional look with some modern twists.

Handknitting Association of Iceland (Handprjónasamband Íslands) (Skólavörðustígur 19, tel. 354/552-1890, www.handknit.is, 9am-6pm Mon.-Fri., 9am-4pm Sat., 11am-4pm Sun.) is a collective of Icelanders that knit and sell sweaters, scarves, shawls, hats, mittens, and other woolen goods. If you are looking for an authentic, traditional Icelandic sweater, and are willing to pay top dollar, this is your place. There are a lot of colors and patterns to choose from in an array of sizes.

Kolaportið (Tryggvagata 19, tel. 354/562-5030, www.kolaportid.is, 11am-5pm Sat.-Sun.) is Reykjavík's only flea market, and, boy, do they go all out in this space. You can find everything from secondhand traditional Icelandic sweaters to used CDs and vinyl records to books and even fresh and frozen fish. A very popular place, it's usually packed, regardless of the weather or season.

KronKron (Laugavegur 63b, tel. 354/562-8388, www.kronkron.com, 10am-6pm Mon.-Thurs., 10am-6:30pm Fri., 10am-5pm Sat.) is a hip shop that focuses on up-and-coming designers. Fashions for men and women range from fun and flirty to chic and modern. You can find elegant dresses,

Handknitting Association of Iceland

fashion-forward sweaters, and unique accessories. The clientele ranges from teens to young professionals, which shows the range of duds available.

GIFTS AND SOUVENIRS

Álafoss (Laugavegur 8, tel. 354/562-6303, www.alafoss.is, 9am-10pm daily) is best known for its huge factory wool store in the Reykjavík suburb of Mosfellsbær, but this small downtown outpost is great for picking up yarn for knitting projects and small wool souvenirs to bring home. You can find socks, hats, magnets, shot glasses, soft toys, candy, and handmade Icelandic soap, among many other goodies.

Blue Lagoon (Laugavegur 15, tel. 354/420-8849, www.bluelagoon.com, 10am-6pm Mon.-Fri., 10am-4pm Sat., 1pm-5pm Sun.) is a tiny shop on the main street that carries all of the Blue Lagoon's skin-care line. If you can't make it to the actual Blue Lagoon near Grindavík, don't fret, because you can take home some of the essence that makes the site so special. The shop is decked out in cool blue hues and lots of lava stones, and the shelves are filled with everything from a nourishing algae mask to mineral bath salts.

The Little Christmas Shop (Laugavegur 8, tel. 354/552-2412, 10am-6pm Mon.-Fri., 10am-5pm Sat., 10:30am-2pm Sun.) is a small shop where it's Christmas all year round. A pair of stone Santa shoes outside the store draws you into a world of Christmas tree ornaments, ceramic Yule Lads figurines, soft toys, dishes, and just about everything with a Christmas theme. No matter what the season, it's a joyous shop to visit and will get you buying Christmas ornaments in July.

Polar Bear Gift Store (Laugavegur 38, tel. 354/578-6020, www.isb-jorninn.is, 10am-8pm daily) is bound to catch your attention with its huge toy polar bear models outside the store. While polar bears are not indigenous to Iceland, don't let that fact stop you from checking out the cute wares inside. You can pick up T-shirts, hats, magnets, keychains, and other souvenirs.

The Little Christmas Shop

Ravens (Laugavegur 15, tel. 354/551-1080, www.ravens.is, 10am-7pm Mon.-Sat., 11am-5pm Sun.) is a unique shop that houses all sorts of good stuff that you can't find anywhere else. You can find arctic fur, authentic Inuit art, lambskin rugs, custom-made knives, sculptures, and leather accessories. You won't find mass-produced souvenirs here.

The Viking (Hafnarstræti 3, tel. 354/551-1250, www.theviking.is, 9am-7pm Mon.-Fri., 9am-6pm Sat.-Sun.) is exactly what you would expect from a souvenir shop in Reykjavík. T-shirts, mugs, stuffed puffins and polar bears, wool products, Viking helmets, and just about everything in between can be found here. If you're looking for unique and sophisticated trinkets, this isn't your spot. But, if you're up for fun and affordable items, you will likely find them here.

Vínberið (Laugavegur 43, tel. 354/551-2475, 9am-6pm Mon.-Fri., 10am-6pm Sat., noon-5pm Sun.) is a sweets shop stocked with everything from chocolates to rhubarb toffee. There's a good mix of local and foreign brands, and it would be almost impossible to not find something you like. Gift options include treats wrapped in pretty packaging. In the back there are spices and baking products, and in the summer there is frequently a mini outdoor fruit market just outside the shop. One sweet that is wildly popular among Icelanders is black licorice. You can find a selection of licorice candies with or without a chocolate coating.

SHOPPING MALLS

Kringlan (Kringlunni 4-12, tel. 354/568-9200, www.kringlan.is, 10am-6:30pm Mon.-Wed., 10am-9pm Thurs., 10am-7pm Fri., 10am-5pm Sat.-Sun.) resembles just about any mall in America. There are clothing stores, a bank, a movie theater, and a food court packed with teenagers and shoppers. If the weather is particularly bad and you want to get some shopping done, it's a good destination. There's a 66 North shop in Kringlan, as well as some other Icelandic brands. Kringlan is a five-minute drive east from downtown Reykjavík, and it can be reached by Strætó bus numbers 1, 2, 3, 4, 6, 13, and 14. One-way bus fare is 350ISK, and it takes about 10 minutes from downtown Reykjavík.

Smáralind (Hagasmári 1, tel. 354/528-8000, www.smaralind.is, 11am-7pm Mon.-Thurs., 11am-9pm Fri., 11am-6pm Sat., 1pm-6pm Sun.) is located in the Reykjavík suburb Kópavogur and is one of the main shopping centers in the region for locals. You will find everything from Adidas sneakers to Levi's, but for double the price than back home. However, it offers a movie theater and an entertainment area with rides for kids if that strikes your fancy.

Reykjavík's culinary charm may be surprising to some. While there are traditional Icelandic restaurants serving up fresh fish and tender lamb fillets, there are also fantastic eateries specializing in food you may not expect to see in Iceland. For instance, there's an impressive collection of Asian and Mediterranean restaurants, which have authentic menus that incorporate the great ingredients found in Iceland. If you're in the mood for tapas, there's a place to have an exquisite meal. Craving sushi? You will not be disappointed. As for Icelandic cuisine, there are upmarket restaurants catering to foodies as well as fast-food joints offering quick, affordable bites.

ICELANDIC

Bergsson Mathús (Templarasund 3, tel. 354/571-1822, www.bergsson.is, 7am-10pm daily, 2,400ISK) is known for its fantastic brunch menu and light, flavorful dishes. Try the roast beef on a bed of salad or the spinach lasagna. The eatery is also a popular coffee spot for locals.

Fjalakötturinn (Aðalstræti 16, tel. 354/514-6060, www.fjalakotturinn.is, lunch 11:30am-2pm daily, dinner 6pm-10pm Sun.-Thurs., 6pm-11pm Fri.-Sat., 3,800ISK) is housed inside Hotel Centrum in downtown Reykjavík, but it's not only a popular place for hotel guests to visit. The inventive food, modern decor, intimate tables, and gorgeous pictures of Iceland's landscape make this spot a winner. Fresh fish including salmon, trout, catfish, and lobster is on the menu, as is rack of lamb.

Iðnó (Vonarstræti 3, tel. 354/562-9700, www.idno.is, noon-10pm daily, 3-course menu from 7,900ISK) is a historic building that houses local theater productions as well as a fine restaurant. Situated close to Tjörnin and the city hall, the restaurant is pricey, but the food is memorable. The smoked salmon on blinis with caviar is exquisite, as is the ginger-glazed breast of duck.

★ **Lækjarbrekka** (Bankastræti 2, tel. 354/551-4430, www.laekjarbrekka.is, 11:30am-10pm daily, entrées from 3,800ISK) occupies a historic building that dates back to 1834. Today, Lækjarbrekka is one of the best-known downtown restaurants catering to tourists. Fresh fish dishes are on the menu alongside some of Iceland's most adventurous cuisine. You'll find fermented shark, whale meat, puffin, and Icelandic horse fillets on offer. For tamer choices, the pan-fried fillet of lamb and arctic char are splendid.

Restaurant Reykjavík (Vesturgata 2, tel. 354/552-3030, www.restaurantreykjavik.is, 11:30am-10pm daily, entrées from 4,000ISK) is known for its fantastic fish buffet (6,950ISK), which starts every day at 6pm. This is a favorite among tourists looking to sample traditional Icelandic fish dishes as well as international classics. The restaurant is housed in a huge yellow building with lots of seating, so you're not likely to have to wait for a table. The fish buffet features everything from salmon, cod, lobster, fish balls, trout, and caviar to shrimp and crab specialties. An à la carte menu offers beef, lamb, fish, and vegetarian options.

Icelandic Bar (Íslenski Barinn) (Ingólfsstræti 1, tel. 354/517-6767, www. islenskibarinn.is, 11:30am-1am Sun.-Thurs., 11:30am-3am Fri.-Sat., entrées from 2,600ISK) takes classic Icelandic ingredients like lamb, whale, and puffin and puts a creative spin on the dishes with interesting flavor combinations. For example, the restaurant serves a sweet and savory dish of grilled puffin with blueberries, pickled red onions, *skyr*, and herbs. Guests can also order items like local salmon, traditional lamb meat soup, and the famous Icelandic hot dog. The reindeer burger is highly recommended.

Matur og Drykkur (Grandagarður 2, tel. 354/571-8877, www.maturog-drykkur.is, 11:30am-10:30pm daily, entrées from 3,200ISK) has an eclectic menu that includes items such as double-smoked lamb with buttermilk and nutmeg, a whole cod's head cooked in chicken stock with dulse (a type of seaweed), and rutabaga soup with red beet caviar and sunflower seeds. The restaurant, which is housed in the Saga Museum, has a casual atmosphere with reminders of the fishing industry—appropriate, because the building used to be a saltfish factory.

★ **Dill Restaurant** (Hverfisgata 12, tel. 354/552-1522, www.dillrestau-rant.is, 6pm-10pm Wed.-Sat., entrées from 11,900) is Iceland's first restaurant to receive a Michelin star and has been a hit with tourists and locals for years. The rotating menu features meat, fish, and creative vegetarian options. Decor is minimalist, allowing the food to take center stage. Be sure to book a table far in advance (at least six weeks), as this is the toughest reservation in Iceland. You can book online or by phone; groups of eight or more must email the restaurant (dillrestaurant@dillrestaurant.is).

SEAFOOD

★ **Fish Market** (Aðlstræti 12, tel. 354/578-8877, www.fiskmarkadurinn. is, 5pm-11pm daily, entrées from 5,100ISK) stands out among a number of fantastic seafood restaurants in Reykjavík. What makes Fish Market special is the way the chef combines ingredients. The grilled monkfish comes with crispy bacon, cottage cheese, tomato yuzu pesto, and crunchy enoki mushrooms. It's a vision, as is the salted cod with lime zest with potato puree, dried cranberries, and celery salad.

Fiskfelagid (Fish Company) (Vesturgata 2a, tel. 354/552-5300, www. fiskfelagid.is, 11:30am-10:30pm Mon.-Thurs., 11:30am-11:30pm Fri., 5:30pm-10:30pm Sat.-Sun., entrées from 4,600ISK) has a striking, chic interior with modern wooden tables and chairs, candleholders throughout the space, and personal notes and photos adorning the walls. There are comfortable couches in the lounge, where you're welcome to sip a cocktail while waiting for a table. The food is flawless, ranging from pan-fried prime lamb and oxtail with artichoke puree to blackened monkfish and fried langoustine with lobster spring rolls.

The Lobster House (Amtmannsstígur 1, tel. 354/561-3303, www.th-elobsterhouse.is, 11:30am-10pm Mon.-Sat., 5pm-10pm Sun., entrées from 4,400ISK) is the place for—you guessed it—lobster. You can't make a bad choice: grilled lobster tails with garlic butter, lobster soup, slow-cooked monkfish and smoked lobster with potato salad, lobster tempura, and lots of other options. If you're not a fan of lobster, don't fret. There are lamb, pork, and other fish options on the menu.

Icelandic Fish & Chips (Tryggvagata 11, tel. 354/551-1118, www.fishand-chips.is, 11:30am-9pm daily, entrées from 1,390ISK) serves up a wonderful range of fresh seafood: cod, plaice, blue ling, haddock, redfish, wolffish, and shellfish. For an authentic Icelandic fish-and-chips meal, go for the cod. The biggest draws, however, are the "skyronnaise dips," in which Iceland's famous soft cheese, *skyr,* is blended with an array of spices, including basil, coriander, ginger, and tarragon. The truffle and tarragon dip is heavenly.

MAR Restaurant (Geirsgata 9, tel. 354/519-5050, www.marrestaurant. com, 11:30am-11pm daily, entrées from 2,900ISK) offers South American-inspired dishes ranging from prosciutto-wrapped monkfish with fennel seeds to lamb fillet with leeks, carrots, and beets. The banana crème brûlée with chocolate sorbet is recommended for dessert. The atmosphere is casual, with wood tables and minimalist design, and the harbor location is great.

★ Sea Baron (Sægreifinn) (Geirsgata 8, tel. 354/553-1500, www.saegre-ifinn.is, 11:30am-10pm daily, entrées from 1,600ISK) has been a Reykjavík institution for years. With its prime location by the harbor, the Sea Baron is known for its perfectly spiced, fresh lobster soup, which comes with a side of bread and butter. Fish kebabs on offer include scallops, monkfish, and cod. Whale meat is also available if you're so inclined. Inside, visitors will find a hut-like atmosphere with fishing relics, photos, and equipment. A net hangs from the ceiling, and charming knickknacks are displayed.

ASIAN

Bambus (Borgartún 16, tel. 354/517-0123, www.bambusrestaurant.is, 11:30am-11pm Mon.-Fri., 5pm-10pm Sat.-Sun., entrées from 1,750ISK) is a delightful Asian fusion restaurant mixing Thai, Japanese, and Indian influences. Dishes incorporate everything from curry to teriyaki and coconut milk. A salad with chicken, sweet chili, and mango is spectacular. The restaurant is decorated in minimalist, Asian-influenced style.

Gandhi Restaurant (Posthusstræti 17, tel. 354/511-1691, www.gandhi. is, 5:30pm-10pm daily, entrées from 3,000ISK) features the creations of two chefs from southwest India. Combining local Icelandic ingredients with traditional Indian spices, the menu offers authentic dishes like chicken vindaloo and fish masala as well as vegetarian options. The food is fresh and perfectly spiced. The butter chicken is gorgeous, rivaling that of the top Indian restaurants in London.

Krua Thai (Skólavörðustígur 21, tel. 354/551-0833, www.kruathai. is, 11:30am-9:30pm Mon.-Fri., noon-9:30pm Sat., 5pm-9:30pm Sun., 1,500ISK) has all your favorite Thai classics, ranging from chicken pad thai to spring rolls and noodle soups. During weekdays, the restaurant has a three-course lunch special for just 1,400ISK.

Noodle Station (Laugavegur 103, tel. 354/551-3198, 11am-10pm daily,

1,580ISK) is a popular spot for Reykjavík natives, students, and tourists. People flock to the tiny shop for one of the tastiest and cheapest meals you can find in downtown. Noodle soup is available with chicken or beef or as a vegetarian option. The smell of spices wafting down Skólavörðustígur will draw you in.

Osushi (Pósthússtræti 13, tel. 354/561-0562, www.osushi.is, 11:30am-10pm Mon.-Thurs., 11:30am-11pm Fri.-Sat., 3pm-10pm Sun., bites 300-500ISK) is a sushi train with bites snaking their way around. Diners are treated to everything from deep-fried shrimp tempura rolls to tuna sashimi and grilled eel bites. For kids, there are chicken teriyaki kebabs, spring rolls, and even a chocolate mousse for dessert.

Ramen Momo (Tryggvagata 16, tel. 354/571-0646, www.ramenmomo. is, 11am-10pm daily, 1,890ISK) is an adorable hidden restaurant not too far from the harbor. Owned and operated by a Tibetan immigrant, Ramen Momo serves up glorious chicken, beef, or vegetarian ramen soup and dumplings. The nondescript eatery has an authentic feel to it, and your taste buds will thank you.

Sushibarinn (Laugavegur 2, tel. 354/552-4444, www.sushibarinn. is, 11:30am-10pm Mon.-Sat., 5pm-10pm Sun., rolls from 1,990ISK) has not only sushi roll staples like California, volcano, and shrimp tempura rolls, but also some creative combinations, including the Rice Against the Machine roll, which has salmon, cream cheese, red onions, and chili. For those who are inclined, whale sushi is on the menu as well.

Sushi Social (Þingholtsstræti 5, tel. 354/568-6600, www.sushisamba. is, 5pm-11pm Sun.-Thurs., 5pm-midnight Fri.-Sat., rolls from 2,500ISK) combines Japanese and South American elements to create inventive and delicious sushi rolls and entrées. You'll find traditional fresh seafood like tuna, salmon, crab, lobster, and shrimp, along with South American influences like spicy salsa, jalapeño mayo, and chimichurri. Main entrées include baked vanilla-infused cod and grilled beef tenderloin with mushroom sauce, jalapeño, and coriander.

MEDITERRANEAN

Gamla Smiðjan (Lækjargata 8, tel. 354/578-8555, www.gamlasmidjan.is, 11:30am-11pm daily, large pizzas from 1,990ISK) is a wildly popular pizza place among the locals, which is telling. While Reykjavík isn't known for its pizza, this place is pretty darn good. You have a choice of an obscene number of toppings, ranging from classic pepperoni to more exotic options like tuna fish and banana. It has a laid-back atmosphere and decent service.

Hornið (Hafnartsræti 15, tel. 354/551-3340, www.hornid.is, 11am-11:30pm daily, large pizzas from 1,890ISK), with its yellow and blue walls, looks like a bistro from the outside, and the interior reveals a relaxed atmosphere with friendly service and yummy pizzas. Classic pizzas include pepperoni, four cheese, and vegetable, but there are also adventurous creations like the Pizza Pecatore, which has shrimp, mussels, and scallops on top. If you're not up for pizza, entrées include salted cod with risotto and fillet of lamb with vegetables.

Ítalía (Laugavegur 11, tel. 354/552-4630, www.italia.is, 11:30am-11pm daily, pasta dishes from 2,900ISK) is a cute Italian restaurant right on the main street, Laugavegur. The menu offers classics like spaghetti Bolognese, lasagna, and mushroom ravioli as well as options that incorporate local ingredients, like smoked salmon with toasted bread and pan-fried salted cod with onions. Pizza and calzones are also on the menu.

FOOD

Tapas Barinn (Vesturgata 3b, tel. 354/551-2344, www.tapas.is, 5pm-11:30pm Sun.-Thurs., 5pm-1am Fri.-Sat., 4,990ISK) has many delightful choices, but if you'd like to taste its best Icelandic dishes, go for the "gourmet feast" in which the chef prepares dishes with smoked puffin, Icelandic sea trout, lobster tails, grilled Icelandic lamb, minke whale with cranberry sauce, and pan-fried blue ling with lobster sauce. The seven plates, along with a shot of the famous Icelandic spirit Brennivin and a chocolate *skyr* mousse dessert, will only set you back 7,990ISK. If you would like more traditional tapas, there are lots of options, including salmon and bacon-wrapped scallop bites.

STEAK HOUSES

Argentina (Barónsstígur 11A, tel. 354/551-9555, www.argentina.is, 4pm-midnight Sun.-Thurs., 4pm-1am Fri.-Sat., entrées from 4,550ISK) is warm and inviting the second you step through the door, with leather couches, a roaring fireplace, and the smell of choice cuts of meat wafting through the air. You can choose from rib eye, T-bone, slow-cooked ox flank, beef rump, porterhouse, and peppered beef tenderloin, among other cuts. Chicken, lamb, and seafood round out the menu, and there is an excellent wine list.

Steikhúsið (Tryggvagata 4, tel. 354/561-1111, www.steik.is, 5pm-10pm Sun.-Wed., 5pm-11pm Thurs.-Sat., steaks from 3,990ISK) has made a big impact on Reykjavík's restaurant scene. Guests can choose from beef rib eye, porterhouse, and T-bone cuts or lamb fillets, with tasty sauces including béarnaise, creamy pepper, and blue cheese. There are also fish entrées on offer as well as a dynamite hamburger with brie, pickled vegetables, mango chutney, chipotle, and bacon. For the adventurous, the surf-and-turf features minke whale and horse meat grilled in a coal oven.

★ Grillmarket (Grillmarkaðurinn) (Lækjargata 2a, tel. 354/571-7777, www.grillmarkadurinn.is, 11:30am-11pm daily, entrées from 4,800ISK) is an upscale restaurant specializing in all things meat. Expect dishes like grilled rack of lamb, dry-aged rib eye steaks, and beef tenderloin. But the restaurant also offers spectacular fish courses like salmon, cod, and fresh langoustine tails. The decor is modern yet rustic with Scandinavian design and a lot of wood. If you are after a top-notch carnivore's dinner, this is your place.

VEGETARIAN

Gló (Engjateigi 19, tel. 354/553-1111, www.glo.is, 11am-9pm daily, 2,500ISK) has a spectacular menu featuring not just vegetarian and vegan options, but also a killer raw food selection. Expect to see staples like tofu and hummus served in creative ways, and there's also an excellent salad bar. The meat dish option can be great if you're traveling with a carnivore. The decor is modern and chic and the staff friendly.

Kaffi Vinyl (Hverfisgata 76, tel. 354/537-1332, 8am-11pm daily, 1,200ISK) is a vegan café and one of the hippest places to hang out in downtown Reykjavík. Music is always playing, and artists and musicians mingle among tourists and locals. Stop by to enjoy tasty coffee drinks, beers, and light meals.

Garðurinn (Klapparstigur 37, tel. 354/561-2345, 11am-8pm Mon.-Fri., noon-5pm Sat.) is a lovely café inhabiting a quiet corner downtown. It has an eclectic rotating menu of vegetarian meals including items like curry, vegetable chili, and lentil patties, all at affordable prices. You can also expect soups, sandwiches, cakes, teas, and coffee.

FAST FOOD

You have to visit ★ **Bæjarins Beztu Pylsur (The Town's Best Hot Dog)** (Tryggvatagata 1, tel. 354/511-1566, www.bbp.is, 10am-1am Sun.-Thurs., 10am-4:30am Fri.-Sat., 450ISK). Even if you don't eat hot dogs, you should get a look at the tiny shack that has long been delighting tourists, locals, food critics, and even U.S. president Bill Clinton. Located close to the harbor, the hot dog stand serves up lamb meat hot dogs, with fresh buns and an array of toppings. If you're out for a late-night bar crawl and get hungry, the stand is open until 4am on weekends.

Grillhusið (Tryggvagata 20, tel. 354/562-3456, www.grillhusid.is, 11:30am-10pm Sun.-Thurs., 11:30am-11pm Fri.-Sat., 2,500ISK) is part diner, part TGI Friday's, with Americana displayed on the walls and an extensive menu ranging from hamburgers to fish-and-chips to salads and sandwiches. There is an interesting array of burgers on offer, and the lamb and béarnaise burger is a personal favorite.

Hamborgara Búllan (Geirsgata 1, tel. 354/511-888, www.bullan.is, 11:30am-9pm daily, burgers from 990ISK) is a corner burger joint situated in the old harbor district, close to where the whale-watching tours depart. The food is tasty, the service quick, and the decor a little kitschy, making this a great spot to grab a quick bite to eat. A special includes a hamburger, fries, and soda for 1,590ISK, which is pretty cheap for a meal in downtown Reykjavík.

Hlölla Bátar (Ingólfstorg, tel. 354/511-3500, www.hlollabatar.is, 11:30am-10pm daily, sandwiches from 1,590ISK) has hot and cold hero/hoagie sandwiches on offer, including barbecue, curry, ham and cheese, and veggie boats. It's a great place to get something quick and fuel up before you continue exploring the city.

Icelandic Hamburger Factory (Islenska Hamborgarafabrikkan)

(Höfðatún 2, tel. 354/575-7575, www.fabrikkan.is, 11am-10pm Sun.-Thurs., 11am-midnight Fri.-Sat., burgers from 2,195ISK) is a wildly popular hamburger joint. It has the look and feel of a casual eatery, but the hamburgers are pretty special. They range from classic hamburgers with lettuce, cheese, and tomatoes to more creative concoctions like the surf-and-turf, which combines a beef patty with tiger prawns, garlic, Japanese seaweed, cheese, lettuce, tomatoes, red onions, and garlic-cheese sauce. Other options include chicken and lamb, as well as a whale meat burger.

Roadhouse (Snorrabraut 56, tel. 354/571-4200, www.roadhouse.is, 11:30am-9:30pm Mon.-Thurs., 11:30am-11pm Fri.-Sat., noon-9:30pm Sun., burgers from 2,395ISK) does its best to depict an American-style hamburger joint. It's kitschy, cute, and familiar, with Americana hanging on the walls, ranging from old license plates to Elvis Presley posters. The food is exceptional "fast food," with choice burgers featuring everything from crumbled blue cheese to jalapeños and fried onions. A favorite among Icelanders is the Texas mac-and-cheese burger, with a patty, macaroni and cheese, bacon, and barbecue sauce piled on top. The pork baby-back ribs are memorable.

CAFÉS

Café Babalu (Skólavörðustígur 22, tel. 354/555-8845, www.babalu.is, 11am-11pm daily, 1,200ISK) is a charming coffeehouse decorated with vintage wood furnishings and kitschy knickknacks. Other than coffee drinks, the two-floor café serves light meals including soup, panini, and crepes. This is a favorite among tourists, and in the summer months, there's an outdoor eating area on the 2nd floor.

Café Haiti (Geirsgata 7, tel. 354/588-8484, www.cafehaiti.is, 6am-9pm Mon.-Thurs., 6am-10pm Fri., 7am-10pm Sat., 7am-8pm Sun., light meals from 1,990ISK) is owned and operated by a delightful Haitian woman who has called Iceland home for years. The atmosphere is warm and inviting,

Café Babalu

with comfortable couches and chairs among the tables and even a little stage area up front hosting regular concerts. In addition to coffee and tea, light meals of soup and sandwiches are available, as well as sweet treats like cakes and cookies. A house favorite is specially brewed Arabic coffee that takes some time, but it's well worth the wait.

C Is for Cookie (Tysgata 8, tel. 354/578-5914, 7:30am-6pm Mon.-Fri., 10am-5pm Sat., 11am-5pm Sun., 500ISK) is a nondescript café on a quiet side street in the city. For that reason, along with a stellar cup of coffee, it's a favorite among locals. When the weather is good, people congregate in a park adjacent to the coffeehouse and at tables and chairs outside. Freshly baked treats include Icelandic pancakes, brownies, and, of course, cookies.

Kaffitár (Bankastræti 8, tel. 354/511-4540, www.kaffitar.is, 7am-6pm daily, 500ISK) is the closest thing Iceland has to a coffee chain like Starbucks. There are locations in the city center, Keflavík airport, and a smattering of other sites. They also sell coffee beans and ground coffee in supermarkets and takeout coffee at gas stations. The city-center location is bright, colorful, and usually crowded. The coffee is fresh and the cakes and other sweets are delicious. You can't go wrong at Kaffitár.

Mokka (Skólavörðustígur 3A, tel. 354/552-1174, www.mokka.is, 9am-6:30pm daily, 500ISK) is the oldest coffeehouse in Reykjavík and retains a faithful following. It's busy all day, with tourists as well as artists, writers, and other folks stopping by for a cup of coffee and Mokka's famous waffles with fresh cream and homemade jam. Art and photography exhibitions are frequently held at the coffeehouse, so stop by and have a look at the walls.

Reykjavík Roasters (Karastigur 1, tel. 354/517-5535, www.reykjavikroasters.is, 8am-6pm Mon.-Fri., 9am-5pm Sat.-Sun., 500ISK) is a charming corner coffeehouse situated in a great part of town. Just a stone's throw from Hallgrímskirkja, Reykjavík Roasters is a wonderful spot to sit down for a coffee to break up a busy day of sightseeing. Decorated with vintage couches and chairs and wood tables with delicate tablecloths, the

Mokka

coffeehouse is packed with tourists and locals chilling out, drinking lattes, and taking advantage of the free Wi-Fi. During the summer months, when the weather is cooperating, there's an outside sitting area where guests can enjoy their drinks while soaking in the sun.

Stofan Café (Vesturgata 3, tel. 354/863-8583, 9am-11pm Mon.-Wed., 9am-midnight Fri.-Sun., 9am-10pm Sun., 500ISK), a hot spot near the harbor, has plenty of couches, chairs, and tables to accommodate its legion of fans. The café serves coffee drinks, local beers, and cakes and light meals. It's common to catch locals enjoying their drinks while curling up with a good book on a vintage armchair.

Brauð & Co (Frakkastígur 16, tel. 354/456-7777, 6am-6pm daily) is the hippest bakery in Reykjavík. You can get great pastries, breads, and cookies, as well as a delicious cup of coffee, plus do some fun people-watching in the heart of downtown. Many of the employees and owners are connected to the music industry.

Sandholt (Laugavegur 36, tel. 354/551-3524, www.sandholt.is, 6:30am-9pm daily) is a lovely place to have a coffee and fresh-baked pastry, sandwich, or panini. The bakery also has fine chocolates and other packaged goodies, like jams and cookies, which make good souvenirs.

ICE CREAM

Eldur og Is (Skólavörðustígur 2, tel. 354/571-2480, 8:30am-11pm daily, 1,000ISK) offers soft-serve and Italian-style ice cream with flavors including the basics: vanilla, chocolate, and strawberry, as well as coffee, pistachio, and several others. A crepe bar inside has delicious combinations, including the Nutella and nut special crepe. This place has a central location and a good reputation, so it can be a bit crowded. The sofas and armchairs inside make it very comfortable.

Ísbúðin Valdís (Grandagarður 21, tel. 354/586-8088, www.valdis.is, 11:30am-11pm daily, from 450ISK) draws a crowd during sun-soaked summer days and the dim, windy dog days of winter. It's always busy here and for good reason. The harbor location and its creative and delicious ice cream flavors make this a favorite among locals and tourists. Flavors include coconut, white chocolate, vanilla coffee, Oreo, and local favorites black licorice and rhubarb. During the summer, there are tables and chairs outside the shop, where scores of people enjoy their cones.

Accommodations

Accommodations in Reykjavík fall into three categories: hotels, guesthouses, and self-catering apartments. The city isn't known for luxurious hotels, but there are a few "upmarket" choices; however, they remain "no-frills" when compared to other cities in Europe. By and large, expect to pay a lot during the high season (June-August). While most of the options are downtown, there are a few outside the 101 postal code. However, given how small Reykjavík is, most options are within walking distance or are within a short bus ride to downtown.

HOTELS

Under 25,000ISK

Fosshótel Baron (Baronsstígur 2-4, tel. 354/562-3204, www.fosshotel.is, rooms from 21,000ISK) may not be pretty from the exterior, but it's clean, convenient, and in a good location in downtown Reykjavík. The 120 rooms range from standard singles and doubles to apartment-style accommodations that have kitchenettes and mini refrigerators. The lobby looks a little depressing, but the accommodating staff and the location make up for it. Guests have access to free Wi-Fi, free and plentiful parking, and an adequate included breakfast.

Hilton Reykjavík Nordica (Suðurlandsbraut 2, tel. 354/444-5000, www. hiltonreykjavik.com, rooms from 23,000ISK) is a 252-room four-star hotel situated in the financial district, about a 10-minute walk from downtown Reykjavík. It attracts business travelers as well as families and individuals thanks to its comfortable rooms, top-notch service, luxurious spa, and memorable in-house restaurant, Vox.

★ **Hótel Frón** (Laugavegur 22A, tel. 354/511-4666, www.hotelfron.is, rooms from 20,000ISK) couldn't have picked a better location if it tried. Located on the high street Laugavegur, the hotel has single, double, and apartment-style studios that are clean, bright, and comfortable. The apartments come with small kitchens, and a couple of them feature Jacuzzi bathtubs. It's also conveniently close to the bars on Laugavegur—though this means it can be quite noisy on Friday and Saturday nights.

Hótel Klöpp (Klapparstígur 26, tel. 354/595-8520, www.centerhotels. is, rooms from 18,000ISK) offers fresh rooms on a quiet corner in the city center. Some rooms feature warm, bright hues including red walls, while others are stark white, clean, and cool. All rooms have hardwood floors and small private bathrooms. Guests have access to free Wi-Fi, assistance with booking tours is provided, and the friendly staff even offers a northern lights wake-up service in the winter when the aurora borealis is visible.

Reykjavík Lights Hotel (Suðurlandsbraut 16, tel. 354/513-9000, www. keahotels.is, rooms from 25,000ISK) is a concept design hotel with 105 rooms, including singles, doubles, triples, and group rooms. Just past the reception area is an airy lobby that houses a bar and the common eating area. Rooms are large, featuring Nordic-style decor and luxurious beds. The bathrooms are modern and stark white with showers. Located outside of the city center, it's about a 10-minute walk to downtown.

Radisson Blu Saga Hotel (Hagatorg, tel. 354/525-9900, www.radisson-blu.com, rooms from 24,000ISK) has a dynamite location in the city center, close to the Reykjavík Art Museum and the famous Bæjarins Beztu Plysur hot dog stand. Rooms are larger than average, many with a maritime theme that's charming. Beds are lush, and the 209 rooms are stocked with bath products from Anne Semonin. Amenities include free Wi-Fi, access to the spa and health center, and two in-house restaurants: Grillið for fine dining and Restaurant Skrudur for more casual meals.

Icelandair Hótel Reykjavík Natura (Hlídarfótur, tel. 354/444-4500, www.icelandairhotels.com, rooms from 19,000ISK) pays homage to Reykjavík's rich art culture with murals and sculptures throughout the building. Built in 1964 but renovated in 2012, the hotel has been a favorite among business travelers due to its proximity to the airport and conference facilities. The in-house restaurant Satt offers a delicious breakfast buffet and meals throughout the day. The main attractions, for many, are the indoor swimming pool and Soley Natura Spa, where guests can get massages, manicures, pedicures, and facial treatments. The hotel is a 20-minute walk to downtown Reykjavík, but guests are given free passes for the city bus, which stops just outside the hotel.

Over 25,000ISK

Centrum Plaza Hotel (Aðalstræti 4, tel. 354/595-8500, www.centerhotels. is, rooms from 30,000ISK) is in the heart of Reykjavík. Many of the 180 rooms have spectacular views of the city, but with that comes quite a bit of noise during the weekends. The rooms are cozy and sparsely decorated but clean and bright. The bathrooms are small, with a shower, and each room has a flat-screen TV and free Wi-Fi. The clientele is a mix of business and leisure travelers. A lounge downstairs tends to be sleepy because of the proximity of popular bars downtown.

Award-winning ★ **101 Hotel** (Hverfisgata 10, tel. 354/580-0101, www.101hotel.is, rooms from 59,000ISK) is quite posh for Reykjavík. In 2017, the *Daily Telegraph* named it one of the best luxury hotels in the city. Rooms are cozy and stylish at the same time with a black-and-white color palette, wood floors, and in-room fireplaces. And while the rooms are pricey, the amenities are pretty great. Each room has a large walk-in shower, flat-screen TV with satellite channels, free high-speed Wi-Fi, a CD/DVD player with a Bose iPod sound dock, and bathrobes and slippers. The restaurant offers an eclectic menu with creations ranging from mussels and pommes frites to Icelandic cod with saffron risotto.

Grand Hotel Reykjavík (Sigtún 38, tel. 354/514-8000, www.grand.is, rooms from 27,000ISK) is a huge 311-room high-rise hotel just a few minutes from downtown Reykjavík. This is a favorite among business travelers and conference attendees because the hotel has meeting rooms and conference facilities. The rooms are large, with hardwood floors and comfortable yet uninspiring furnishings. The restaurant is pricey; dishes range from lamb fillets with mushrooms to duck breast with parsnip.

Hlemmur Square (Laugavegur 25, tel. 354/415-1600, www.hlemmur-square.com, rooms from 28,000ISK) bills itself as an upmarket hostel. As the name suggests, the hotel is right next to Hlemmur bus station, which is downtown's most extensive station and provides bus transfers to just about every part of the city. Other than being in a killer location, Hlemmur

Square has a popular lounge that attracts both hotel guests and locals. This is a great spot for twentysomethings to meet fellow travelers and socialize.

★ **Hótel Borg** (Posthússtræti 9-11, tel. 354/551-1440, www.hotelborg.is, rooms from 30,000ISK) is a popular choice for celebrities and politicians passing through Reykjavík. Why? Built in 1930, the 56-room four-star downtown hotel is at once elegant, modern, and steeped in old-time charm. Hotel Borg's rooms have custom-made furniture, flat-screen satellite TVs, and very comfortable beds. The in-house restaurant, Silfur, is a favorite, and a café/bar serves light meals.

Hotel Holt (Bergstaðastæti 37, tel. 354/552-5700, www.holt.is, rooms from 40,000ISK) offers spacious, tastefully decorated rooms, some with a balcony. Holt is one of the few hotels in downtown Reykjavík that offers room service, and its service and amenities are comparable to upscale hotels in large European cities. Guests also have free access to Iceland's largest health club (World Class Fitness), free parking, free Wi-Fi, and a staff eager to assist with tour bookings and recommendations for sights and restaurants.

★ **Icelandair Hótel Reykjavík Marina** (Myrargata 2, tel. 354/560-8000, www.icelandairhotels.com, rooms from 26,000ISK) is in a great location by the harbor district, close to the whale-watching tours, restaurants, and museums. One of the most design conscious of the Icelandair Hótels chain, Reykjavík Marina displays art throughout the lobby, restaurant, and rooms, featuring everything from murals by local Icelandic artists to impressive wood sculptures. Rooms are minimalist and modern, the staff is warm, and the hotel is home to one of the hippest hotel bars in the city, Slipp Bar.

Kvosin Hotel (Kirkutorg 4, tel. 354/571-4460, www.kvosinhotel.is, rooms from 30,000ISK) is a gorgeous modern boutique hotel situated close to the Pond and parliament in downtown Reykjavík. Rooms come in four adorably described sizes: normal, bigger, biggest, and larger than life. All

Hótel Borg

rooms feature mini refrigerators, a Nespresso machine, Samsung Smart TV, and skin-care amenities from Aveda. The rooms are sleek and Scandinavian cool with accents from local Icelandic designers. A delicious breakfast is included and served downstairs at the Bergsson restaurant.

Radisson Blu 1919 Hotel (Posthússtræti 2, tel. 354/599-1000, www.radissonblu.com, rooms from 27,000ISK) is an 88-room hotel that occupies a central location in the capital. Built in 1919, the hotel has undergone a couple of renovations, but it has maintained a lot of its charm. The rooms are large, with hardwood floors, sizable bathrooms, comfortable beds, and free high-speed Wi-Fi. Guests who reserve a suite are treated to a king-size bed, Jacuzzi bathtub, and bathrobe with slippers. Guests also have access to a fitness center with some basic machines. The in-house restaurant is dynamite, with a menu ranging from fresh fish caught off of Iceland's shores to lamb fillets and duck breast entrées.

GUESTHOUSES
Under 25,000ISK

Reykjavik Hostel Village (Flókagata 1, tel. 354/552-1155, www.hostelvillage.is, rooms from 15,000ISK) offers rooms in five different residential houses. Rooms include dorm accommodations, singles, doubles, triples, and apartment-style studios. The decor is simple, with neutral colors and wood furnishings. It's a five-minute walk to Laugavegur, the main drag, and the prices are reasonable, making this a great option for budget travelers.

★ **Loft Hostel** (Bankastræti 7, tel. 354/553-8140, www.lofthostel.is, private rooms from 23,000ISK) has a reputation as a place to see and be seen. Rooms range from dorm accommodation to privates, but the big draw is the 4th-floor bar/café that hosts up-and-coming bands, established live acts, and DJs. An outdoor deck overlooks Bankastræti in downtown Reykjavík, and it's packed with locals and tourists alike when the sun is shining.

Sunna Guesthouse (Thórsgata 26, tel. 354/511-5570, www.sunna.is, rooms from 19,000ISK) offers several types of accommodations: one- and two-bedroom apartments, studios, rooms with private bathrooms, and rooms with shared bathroom facilities. All rooms are decorated in a light, minimalist style with muted colors and wood furniture. The location is key, as it's right across the street from Hallgrímskirkja in downtown Reykjavík. Guests have access to a shared kitchen to prepare meals, and a breakfast buffet is included in the price. The breakfast accommodates vegetarians as well as those with gluten allergies.

★ **Kex Hostel** (Skúlagata 28, tel. 354/561-6060, www.kexhostel.is, private rooms from 22,000ISK) is a lot more than a hostel; it's where music lovers, hipsters, and the beautiful people of downtown Reykjavík congregate, meeting for drinks and live music. The hostel offers options ranging from dorm accommodations to private rooms, all with shared bathroom facilities. That said, most people don't stay for the style or comfort of the rooms, but for the Kex experience. The front lounge houses vintage wall maps, mid-century furniture, and a small stage for live bands to plug in and play. The back room is a converted gym that hosts concerts, fashion and vinyl markets, and even food festivals.

APARTMENTS
Under 25,000ISK

Bolholt Apartments (Bolholt 6, tel. 354/517-4050, www.stay.is, rooms from 18,000ISK) offers comfortable, simple rooms just a 10-minute walk from downtown Reykjavík, which makes this well-managed apartment complex very popular. Guests have private bathrooms, small kitchenettes, and access to free Wi-Fi and free parking. A common lounge has a pool table and a couple of sofas great for unwinding and meeting fellow travelers. Bolholt is an excellent option for independent, budget-conscious travelers.

Einholt Apartments (Einholt 2, tel. 354/517-4050, www.stay.is, rooms from 18,000ISK) has stylish, minimalist apartments with private bathrooms and kitchenettes. Its clientele ranges from more mature travelers to twentysomething backpackers. Einholt is a great downtown spot for the independent traveler to spend a couple of nights or a longer stay to get to know Reykjavík.

The **Reykjavík4You Apartments** (Laugavegur 85, www.reykjavik4you.com, rooms from 25,000ISK) offer great spaces in a central location. Studios and one- and two-bedroom apartments are available, and all are stocked with well-equipped kitchens, spacious bathrooms, and bright decor. Apartments are clean and comfortable, with lots of light in the summer months.

Room with a View (Laugavegur 18, tel. 354/552-7262, www.roomwithaview.is, rooms from 20,000ISK) is right next to the popular bookstore Mál og Menning and near all the great bars downtown. Rooms range from small singles to three-bedroom apartments for groups. Rooms are clean and modern, some with private bathroom facilities. Guests have access to two hot tubs as well as a common kitchen area. Be advised that because of the proximity of bars and restaurants, it can be quite noisy on Friday and Saturday nights. If you're looking for a quiet room on a sleepy street, this isn't it.

Information and Services

VISITORS CENTERS

Reykjavík Official Tourist Information Centre (Tjarnargata 11, tel. 354/411-6040, 8am-8pm daily) is downtown inside Reykjavík City Hall. The office has brochures, a friendly and knowledgeable staff, and maps. You can book excursions from here as well.

MEDIA

The *Reykjavík Grapevine* is Iceland's only English-language newspaper, and it's geared toward tourists, hipsters, and music-loving locals. There are listings for bands and DJ club dates, information about what's on at museums and art galleries, and articles ranging from humorous to informative to sarcastic on what's going on in Reykjavík. To get the pulse of the city, pick up a copy in bookstores, museums, and shops, or check it out online at www.grapevine.is. In summertime, the newspaper comes out every other week, and in the winter it's monthly.

EMERGENCY SERVICES

The telephone number for emergencies is 112. If you are having a medical emergency, are stranded by car trouble, or are experiencing a safety issue or any other pressing, dire emergency, dial this number.

MEDICAL SERVICES

Landspitali (Norðurmýri, tel. 354/543-1000, www.landspitali.is) is the national hospital of Iceland. It houses day-patient units, an emergency room, and clinical services. If you are experiencing a medical emergency, dial 112 for an ambulance.

For a pharmacy, visit **Lyf og Heilsa** (Haaleitisbraut 68, tel. 354/581-2101, 8am-midnight Mon.-Fri., 10am-midnight Sat.-Sun.). Keep in mind that over-the-counter medication and aspirin are only available at a pharmacy, not in supermarkets or convenience stores like in other countries.

Transportation

GETTING THERE

Air

Iceland isn't as difficult to reach as you may think. Smack-dab in the mid-Atlantic, Reykjavík is just a short flight for many North Americans and Europeans, about five hours from New York City and three hours from London. The majority of international travel is handled through **Keflavík International Airport** (KEF), which is about 50 minutes west of Reykjavík.

Reykjavík City Airport (Þorragata 10, tel. 354/569-4100, www.isavia.is) is the city's domestic airport, with regional connections to towns throughout the country, including Akureyri and the Westfjords. The only international flights are to the Faroe Islands and Greenland.

Several airlines have offices in Reykjavík: **Air Iceland Connect** (Reykjavíkurflugvöllur, tel. 354/570-3000, www.airicelandconnect.com), **Eagle Air** (Reykjavíkurflugvöllur, tel. 354/562-4200, www.eagleair.is), **Icelandair** (Reykjavíkurflugvöllur, tel. 354/505-0100, www.icelandair.is), and **Wow Air** (Katrinartun 12, tel. 354/590-3000, www.wowair.is).

The **Fly Bus** (tel. 354/580-5400, www.flybus.is) runs regularly from **Keflavík International Airport** to **BSÍ** (Vatnsmýrarvegur 10, tel. 354/562-1011, www.bsi.is), Reykjavík's main bus station, where you can get a shuttle to the downtown hotels. It takes about 50 minutes to get from Keflavík to BSÍ bus station, and buses depart about 40 minutes after flights land. One-way tickets cost 2,500ISK. (BSÍ is also the main departure site for day-tour bus trips with various companies, including Reykjavík Excursions.) **Taxis** are also available at Keflavík; the fare from the airport to Reykjavík is upward of 15,000ISK.

Strætó (www.straeto) bus numbers 15 and 19 stop at the **Reykjavík City Airport** near the Air Iceland and Eagle Air terminals, respectively. Taxis are also available on-site.

GETTING AROUND
Bus
Reykjavík's bus system is convenient, reliable, and an affordable way to get around the city. The bus system, called **Strætó** (www.straeto.is), which means "street" in Icelandic, runs about 30 bus lines within the city center as well as to outlying areas like Kópavogur and Hafnarfjörður. The bright yellow buses cost 350ISK per ride within the city limits, and you can ask for a free bus transfer if you need to switch buses to get to your destination. You must pay with exact change; bus drivers don't make change. Buses run daily 7am-11pm. Be sure to check the website at www.straeto.is for information on holiday schedules and delays due to weather.

If you plan to use the bus a fair amount, you can buy nine tickets for 3,000ISK at **Hlemmur bus station** (Laugavegur, tel. 354/540-2701). Hlemmur is Strætó's central downtown station, where you can catch or connect to any bus you're looking for. Think of it as Reykjavík's equivalent of New York's Times Square subway station. Another great option is the **Reykjavík Welcome Card**, which grants you free access to the city's swimming pools, almost all the city's museums, and unlimited city bus rides. You can purchase a card for one or three days for 900ISK and 2,200ISK, respectively. If you will be spending a lot of time in Reykjavík, this is a great option to save a lot of money. Cards can be purchased at tourist offices and bus stations.

Strætó's blue long-distance buses depart from **Mjodd station** (tel. 354/557-7854), eight kilometers southeast of the city center, traveling to several regions around the country.

Taxi
The two things you need to know about taxis in Reykjavík is that they are expensive, and you have to call ahead for one (for instance, a ride from the BSI bus station to Harpa takes about eight minutes and costs roughly 2,000ISK). **Hreyfill** (tel. 354/588-5522, www.hreyfill.is) and **BSR** (tel. 354/561-0000, www.taxireykjavik.is) are two popular taxi companies in the city. Taxis arrive 5-10 minutes after you call, and the price on the meter is inclusive—you

don't tip in Iceland. Cab prices rival those in New York City: It's rare to
spend less than 2,000ISK on a taxi ride, even for short distances. There are
a couple of cab stations downtown where you don't have to call ahead—just
outside Hlemmur bus station and near Lækjartorg, a square in downtown
Reykjavík where Lækjargata, Bankastræti, and Austurstræti streets meet.
The taxi stands are hard to miss, as the cabs can be lined up 10 deep.

Car

There is no shortage of companies in Iceland eager to rent you a car, and
many of them make it quite easy, with offices at Keflavík International
Airport, BSÍ bus station, and around the city. They include the follow-
ing: **Avis** (Knarrarvogur 2, tel. 354/591-4000, www.avis.is), **Budget**
(Vatsmýrarvegur 10, tel. 354/562-6060, www.budget.is), **Europcar**
(Hjallahrauni 9, tel. 354/565-3800, www.europcar.is), and **Hertz** (Reykjavík
City Airport, tel. 354/505-0600, www.hertz.is).

Be advised that parking isn't easy in Reykjavík. Most locals have cars,
and street parking can take some time. However, there are several parking
garages and lots available around the city, and parking at a garage will cost
less than 100ISK per hour.

Bicycle

Reykjavík has made great strides in becoming more bicycle friendly over
the past few years. There are new bicycle lanes throughout the city as well
as new bike racks to lock up your ride outside shops. Be aware that bike
theft is rampant, so be proactive and lock up your bicycle; if you leave it
unattended and unlocked, it'll disappear. Other than bike theft, the only
concern for cyclists is weather, which changes often. You can start your
ride during calm and sunny skies, but within minutes that could change
to rain and wind.

In Reykjavík, Wow Air sponsors a **city bike program** (www.wowcity-
bike.com). Visitors can rent the purple bicycles from several kiosks around
the city, including near Laugardalslaug. The station map can be accessed
on the website. Rates start at 350ISK for 30 minutes; an additional 30 minutes costs 500ISK.

Walking

Reykjavík is an inherently walkable city—depending on the weather, of
course. Because of its small size, it's a perfect place to roam, to pop into
quaint shops, visit museums, and photograph its many statues. You can
start at the harbor and make your way to Tjörnin, up to Hallgrímskirkja,
and beyond.

A walking tour by **I Heart Reykjavík** (Mjóahlíð 14, tel. 354/854-4476,
www.iheartreykjavik.net) is designed to tell you about the history of
Reykjavík and some of the quirky characters who inhabit the city. The
three-hour tour is 6,000ISK, and you can book at www.tours.iheartreyk-
javik.net. Tours are offered daily.

MOSFELLSBÆR

Just 15 minutes from downtown Reykjavík, Mosfellsbær is a quaint, placid town with a picturesque bay, beautiful mountains, and clean streams and rivers. About 10,000 people live in Mosfellsbær, and despite its proximity to downtown it feels remote enough to make it seem like you're in the countryside.

Sights

ÁLAFOSS WOOL FACTORY SHOP

The **Álafoss Wool Factory Shop** (Álafossvegur 23, tel. 354/566-6303, www. alafoss.is, 8am-8pm daily) is home to the Álafoss wool brand, which was established in 1896 and was for decades the leading manufacturer and exporter of Icelandic wool products. The shop is located in the old factory house by the Álafoss waterfall, which was used to drive the mills. The shop sells wool skeins, scarves, hats, sweaters, and blankets, along with some other small goods. You can also purchase a sheep skin as well as other Icelandic design products. The prices are comparable to those in downtown Reykjavík, but the selection is better and bigger. The site also includes an exhibition of old knitting machinery and photographs from the mill's early days.

GLJÚFRASTEINN

Gljúfrasteinn (Pósthólf 250, tel. 354/568-8066, www.gljufrasteinn.is, 9am-5pm daily June 1-Aug. 31, 10am-4pm Tues.-Sun. Sept. 1-May 31, 900ISK) was the home of Icelandic novelist and national treasure Halldór Laxness. Halldór, who was awarded the Nobel Prize for Literature in 1955 for his novel *Independent People,* lived at this home from 1945 until his death in 1998. It has been preserved as a museum, giving visitors a glimpse into his life, including the library and study where he wrote several of his works. The white two-story concrete building is well preserved, but it feels lived in with lots of personal artifacts decorating the home, including books, clothing, and furniture. There is a short multimedia presentation about Halldór's life and work, available in English, Icelandic, and Swedish. Guided tours of the house and grounds take about an hour. You can purchase many of his books at the museum, translated into English and German.

Sports and Recreation

★ HIKING MOUNT ESJA

Standing 914 meters high, Mount Esja looms over Reykjavík. It's a favorite among locals and the subject of thousands of picturesque photographs snapped by tourists. Hiking Esja is a popular pastime and a few paths ascend the mountain. The most popular path begins at the car park, which is

Greater Reykjavík

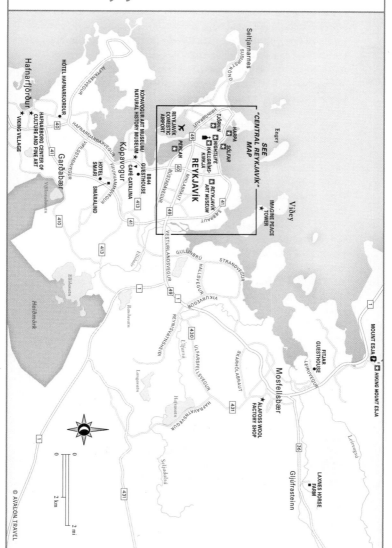

© AVALON TRAVEL

at about 780 meters. From there, you can cross the Mógilsa stream, which leads to a steeper stretch named "steinnin." The hike is eight kilometers round-trip and considered easy, but be aware that the last stretch to the top is pretty steep; there are handrails to lessen the challenge. When you reach the top of this path, you can sign a guestbook. It's fun to read through all the names and see where people have traveled from to climb the mountain. At a leisurely pace, the hike takes about two hours total.

Please take precautions before you head out. Make sure you check the weather forecast and let your guesthouse or hotel know of your plans. Remember that the weather can be fickle. It may be beautiful out with sunny skies, but it could turn very windy and rainy quickly. Bring water, proper footwear, and waterproof clothing with you.

Getting to Esja is pretty easy, even if you don't have access to a car. It's just 20 minutes (10.7 kilometers) north of Mosfellsbær and is accessible from Route 1. Drive through Mosfellsbær and you'll see signs pointing to the car park. You can also take the **Strætó** 57 bus (www.straeto.is) from the bus station Mjodd in Reykjavík. The bus fare is 880ISK and the bus departs 12 times a day. It's a 30-minute ride. Let the bus driver know that you are heading to the base of Esja (the bus stop is Esjumelar) and you will get dropped off at the car park.

HORSE RIDING

If you're staying in Reykjavík and want to do some horseback riding, **Laxnes Farm** (off Rte. 36, tel. 354/566-6179, www.laxnes.is) is just a 15-minute drive northeast from downtown. Icelandic horses are available to ride year-round for different tour lengths. The staff is warm and friendly and shows a great deal of love and respect for the horses they care for. A popular tour is called the "Laxnes Special"; you will be picked up at your hotel or guesthouse in Reykjavík and taken to the farm, where you will meet your guide and horse. You are given all the gear you need, including helmets, rain clothes, and boots, and are taken on a glorious two-hour tour (11,900ISK) that has spectacular landscape views. The Laxnes Farm is close to Halldór Laxness's home, but they are not related.

SWIMMING

If you're planning to stay in town for a few hours or more, check out the local swimming pool, called **Varmárlaug** (Þverholt 2, tel. 354/566-6754, 6:30am-8pm Mon.-Fri., 9am-6pm Sat.-Sun. in summer, 4pm-9pm Mon.-Fri. in winter, 750ISK). The pool isn't as impressive as some of the pools in the Reykjavík city center, but the water is warm and the facilities are clean. You're likely to see locals taking a dip, but not many tourists.

Food and Accommodations

Mosfellsbakarí (Háholti 13-15, tel. 354/566-6145, www.mosbak.is, 7am-6pm Mon.-Fri., 8am-4pm Sat.-Sun., pastries from 600ISK) is a decadent bakery known for its chocolate creations. Located in the center of town, it does a roaring business. In addition to its indulgent cakes and pastries, the bakery offers light meals, including sandwiches and soup.

Fitjar Guesthouse (Fitjar, tel. 354/691-5005, www.fitjarguesthouse. com, rooms from 16,000ISK) is a six-room guesthouse on a quiet street in Mosfellsbær. Three rooms have private bathroom facilities with a shower, and three rooms share bathroom accommodations. Rooms are clean and comfortable, but the decor is nothing to write home about. This is a great spot to spend a night before you continue on your journey. Guests have access to free Wi-Fi, a television, a common room, fully equipped kitchen, and laundry facilities.

Information and Services

Mosfellsbær's **tourist information office** is based inside the **Mosfellsbær public library** (Þverholti 2, tel. 354/566-6822, www.mosfellsbaer.is, 9am-5pm daily), which is housed in a shopping area. It's a great place to gather some tourist brochures and maps as well as buy some food at the grocery store inside the shopping center.

Transportation

Mosfellsbær is just a 15-minute drive from downtown Reykjavík. It's 14 kilometers northeast of Reykjavík via Route 49.

By bus, take the 15 bus to the Haholt stop, which is in the center of town. Check www.straeto.is for more bus information. Depending on the time of day, buses run every 30 minutes to every hour, and it takes 30 minutes from downtown Reykjavík to Mosfellsbær. A single ride on the bus is 440ISK.

KÓPAVOGUR

Kópavogur is a quiet suburb home to families, young professionals, and immigrants, and it attracts people traveling on business or shoppers headed to the Smáralind mall or the island's only IKEA and Costco. There are a couple of museums worth checking out for local art and history.

Sights
KÓPAVOGUR ART MUSEUM
(Gerðarsafn)

The **Kópavogur Art Museum** (Hamraborg 4, tel. 354/570-0440, www. gerdarsafn.is, 11am-5pm Tues.-Sun., 500ISK) is named Gerðarsafn in Icelandic, after sculptor Gerður Helgadóttir, who passed away in 1975. In 1977, her heirs donated roughly 1,400 of her works to the municipality of Kópavogur on the condition that a museum bearing her name would be opened. The museum opened in 1994. Gerður's black-iron works in the 1950s made her a pioneer of three-dimensional abstract art in Iceland. Around 1970 Gerður returned to working with plaster, terra cotta, and concrete, using simple circles with movement in many variations. Other works on display range from contemporary to landscape art. It's a pretty museum with varied works of art, and it's worth a visit if you're in the neighborhood.

NATURAL HISTORY MUSEUM
(Náttúrúfræðistofa)

The **Natural History Museum** (Hamraborg 6A, tel. 354/570-0430, www. natkop.is, 9am-6pm Mon.-Thurs., 11am-5pm Fri.-Sat., free) is a great place to bring kids to learn about the animals and geology of Iceland. The exhibits fall into two categories: zoological and geological. The geology section, where you learn about the major rock types and minerals of Iceland, is of more interest to adults. The zoological part focuses on the mammals, fish, birds, and invertebrates of the country. It's educational and entertaining, and kids love the exhibitions on seals, foxes, and cute birds like puffins.

Sports and Recreation
SWIMMING

The **Kópavogur Swimming Pool** (Borgarholtsbruat 17, tel. 354/540-0470, 6:30am-10pm Mon.-Fri., 8am-7pm Sat.-Sun., 500ISK) is frequented by locals and their children and has a very family-friendly atmosphere. Amenities include a 50-meter outdoor pool, two smaller indoor pools, three waterslides, seven hot pots, and a steam bath. You aren't likely to see crowds or tourists, so if you're looking to just swim, this is a good spot.

Food and Accommodations

Smáralind (Hagasmara 1, tel. 354/528-8000, www.smaralind.is, 11am-7pm Mon., Wed., and Fri., 11am-9pm Thurs., 11am-6pm Sat., 1pm-6pm Sun.) is Iceland's largest shopping mall, and in addition to a food court, there are casual eateries TGI Friday's and Café Adesso, coffee shop Kaffitár, and Serrano, which serves Mexican-style food.

Hótel Smári (Hlíðarsmára, tel. 354/558-1900, www.hotelsmari.is, rooms from 23,000ISK) is a 48-room block hotel situated right next to the huge mall Smáralind. The rooms need an update, as they have a 1980s style with carpeting, orange hues, and shiny lamps. But the rooms are clean and spacious, and comfortable for a short stay.

BB44 Guesthouse (Borgarholtsbraut 44/Nýbýlavegur 16, tel. 354/554 4228, www.bb44.is, doubles 20,800ISK) offers eight guest rooms in two locations. The single, double, and family rooms have free Wi-Fi, shared kitchen facilities, and free parking. Rooms are very basic, with standard beds, desks, and simple chairs. The location is prime, just a 10-minute walk from downtown Kópavogur, where there are museums, restaurants, and the town's swimming pool. Guests have access to a hot tub at the guesthouse.

Information and Services

The town's **service and administration center** (Fannborg 2, tel. 354/570-1500) is open 8am-4pm Monday-Thursday and 8am-3pm Friday.

Transportation

Kópavogur is just a 10-minute ride (5 kilometers) south from downtown Reykjavík by car. You take Route 40 to Route 49.

City buses go to Kópavogur, including buses 1, 2, and 28. Buses leave every 30 minutes or so, the fare is 440ISK one-way, and it takes about 20 minutes by bus. Check www.straeto.is for more bus information.

HAFNARFJÖRÐUR

Hafnarfjörður is a picturesque fishing town that about 30,000 people call home. Attractions include a scenic harbor, pretty parks, and the famous Viking Village, a restaurant and hotel that plays host to numerous Viking-related events.

Sights

HAFNARFJÖRÐUR MUSEUM

Hafnarfjörður Museum (Vesturgata 8, www.hafnarfjordur.is, 11am-5pm daily June 1-Aug. 31, 11am-5pm Sat.-Sun. rest of year, free) houses a collection of cultural artifacts and photographs that are significant to the town. The museum consists of six houses and nine exhibitions that showcase life in the town's early days. The six houses date from 1803 to 1906 and include the oldest house in the town, Sivertsen's House.

HAFNARBORG CENTER OF CULTURE AND FINE ART

Hafnarborg Center of Culture and Fine Art (Strandgata 34, tel. 354/555-0800, www.hafnarborg.is, noon-5pm Wed.-Mon., free) consists of two galleries with rotating exhibitions ranging from contemporary art by modern Icelandic artists to works by some of the island's most celebrated artists of years past.

VIKING VILLAGE
(Fjörukráin)

Viking Village (Strandgata 55, tel. 354/565-1213, www.vikingvillage.is) is great fun for kids and adults alike. The closest thing Iceland has to a theme

Hafnarfjörður

park, the Viking Village celebrates the island's history—with a sense of humor. It's kitschy, with lots of Viking horns, reproduced wood huts, and wooden furnishings. Guests can stay at the hotel, visit the gift shop, stay for a meal at the restaurant, or just check out the decor.

The Viking Village takes center stage every mid-June when the space hosts the **Viking Festival,** which takes place over five days. There are performances of jousts with participants in Viking costumes, food stands, metalwork demonstrations, and woolen goods and jewelry for sale.

Sports and Recreation
HORSE RIDING
This town is a lovely place to ride a horse. With its rolling landscape and picturesque views, it doesn't get much better than this in the greater Reykjavík area. **Íshestar** (Sörlaskeið 26, tel. 354/555-7000, www.ishestar. is) is a local company that offers an array of tours year-round. It provides transportation to the riding center from your accommodation and all gear needed to ride. A half-day tour goes for about 19,500ISK. **Extreme Iceland** (Skutuvogur 13a, tel. 354/588-1300, www.extremeiceland.is, 19,500ISK) also offers a day tour from Hafnarfjörður, with 4-5 hours of riding along the Reykjanes Peninsula.

SWIMMING
Take a dip with the locals at the **Suðurbæjarlaug** pool (Hringbruat 77, tel. 354/565-3080, 6:30am-9:30pm Mon.-Fri., 8am-5:30pm Sat.-Sun., 600ISK), which has an outdoor pool with a waterslide, a steam bath, and a few hot tubs.

Food
Viking Restaurant (Fjörugarðurinn) (Strandagata 55, tel. 354/565-1213, www.fjorukrain.is, 2,400ISK) at the Viking Village is a restaurant that serves traditional Icelandic fare like lamb and fish dishes in a fun, Viking-themed atmosphere. There are lots of wood furnishings and medieval accents displayed throughout the space. You can book a Viking performance in advance for groups of any size for a fee, which includes the guests being "kidnapped" from their bus, brought into a "cave" in the restaurant, served mead, escorted to dinner, and entertained with singing and music. The restaurant is open for dinner 6pm-10pm daily.

Osushi (Reykjarvíkurvegi 60, tel. 354/561-0562, www.osushi.is, 11:30am-9:30pm Mon.-Thurs., 11:30am-10pm Fri.-Sat., 3pm-9:30pm Sun., bites from 400ISK) is the Hafnarfjörður outpost of the popular downtown Reykjavík sushi train. Individual bites on offer range from fresh salmon farmed from Iceland's shores to eel and shrimp-based pieces.

Súfistinn (Strandata 9, tel. 354/565-3740, 8am-11:30pm Mon.-Thurs., 8am-midnight Fri., 10am-midnight Sat., 1pm-midnight Sun., 800ISK) is a cozy café that sells stellar coffee drinks, fresh pastries, and light meals.

Situated by the central downtown shopping area and performance hall, it's a perfect place to grab a blueberry muffin and latte or a soup or sandwich.

Accommodations

Hótel Hafnarfjörður (Reykjavíkurvegur 72, tel. 354/540-9700, www.hho-tel.is, rooms from 26,000ISK) is a 70-room hotel with comfortable rooms ranging from single rooms to family suites. The hotel has a business traveler/corporate feel to it, but you can't beat the amenities and location. Rooms feature neutral hues, simple furnishings, and private bathrooms. Some rooms have a kitchenette for self-catering needs. Continental breakfast, Wi-Fi, parking, and access to a nearby fitness center are included in the price.

Hótel Viking (Strandgata 55, tel. 354/565-1213, www.vikingvillage.is, rooms from 16,000ISK) at the Viking Village has 42 hotel rooms and 14 "Viking cottages" next to the hotel. All rooms and cottages include private bathrooms, comfortable beds, televisions, and stylish Viking accessories. The hotel features artworks from Iceland, Greenland, and the Faroe Islands. Guests have access to free Wi-Fi, free parking, and an on-site hot tub. Breakfast is included in the price.

Information and Services

The tourist information center is situated in **Hafnarfjörður Town Hall** (Strandgata 6, tel. 354/585-5555, www.hafnarfjordur.is, 8am-5pm Mon.-Fri. year-round, 10am-3pm Sat.-Sun. June-Aug.). You can arrange for transportation, buy tickets to local tours, and peruse brochures about the town's sights.

Transportation

Hafnarfjörður is just a 15-minute drive (11 kilometers) south from downtown Reykjavík. Take Route 40 to get there.

City bus 1 stops in town. Check www.straeto.is for bus schedules and information.

VIÐEY ISLAND

Viðey is a little gem of an island accessible by ferry. Historically, the island was inhabited by an Augustine monastery from 1225 to 1539 and was a pilgrimage destination in the Middle Ages. The island is home to one of the oldest buildings in Iceland—**Viðeyjarstofa** (Höfuðborgarsvæði), which dates back to 1755 and served as a home to many of Iceland's most powerful men over generations. The building, made from white stone with a black roof, is open to the public. The island, which is just 1.6 square kilometers in size, hosts unspoiled nature with vast stretches of grassy plains and rich birdlife, as well as the Imagine Peace Tower, an installation created by Yoko Ono.

Imagine Peace Tower

The **Imagine Peace Tower** (www.imaginepeacetower.com) is an outdoor installation created by artist Yoko Ono in memory of her late husband, John Lennon. Ono chose Iceland because it's one of the most peaceful countries in the world. The base of the tower is 10 meters wide, and the words "imagine peace" are inscribed on the structure in 24 languages. A vertical beam of light shines from the structure 4,000 meters into the sky and is visible from miles away. It was unveiled on October 9, 2007, Lennon's 67th birthday. It's lit every year October 9-December 8, the latter of which is the anniversary of Lennon's death.

Transportation

In the summer, **Elding** (tel. 354/533-5055, www.videy.com) operates a ferry with eight daily departures mid-May through September from Skarfabakki pier, Harpa, and Ægisgarður pier. Ferries run in the afternoon. During the rest of the year the ferry runs three departures on Saturdays and Sundays from Skarfabakki to Viðey. The ferry ride costs 1,500ISK for adults or 750ISK for children 7-17, and takes about 10 minutes.

Viðey Island

The Reykjanes Peninsula is home to a striking, dramatic landscape comprising lava fields, volcanic craters, geothermal waters and hot springs, and lava caves. The region is also a hotbed for outdoor activities, including horse riding, ATV riding, and bathing in hot springs.

REYKJANESBÆR (KEFLAVÍK AND NJARÐVÍK)

Reykjanesbær is where every tourist's journey begins in Iceland, as it is home to the country's only international airport, Keflavík.

During World War II, British and American troops arrived in Iceland and built the country's first air base. Situated in between the United States and continental Europe, Iceland's location served the Allies well. Some may be surprised to learn that the last American troops left the island only in 2006.

While it may be tempting to get off the plane and get on a bus straight to Reykjavík, Reykjanesbær, which is a municipality that includes the towns **Keflavík** and **Njarðvík**, is a great place to explore. The region's lava fields, majestic sea cliffs, and accessible hiking trails make it a perfect place to roam. Throw on some hiking boots and have your camera ready. It's also a great spot for bird-watching during the summer months, when you can see arctic terns and gannets.

Sights

REYKJANES HERITAGE MUSEUM

Reykjanes Heritage Museum (Duusgata 2-8, Keflavík, tel. 354/421-6700, noon-5pm daily, 1,500ISK) hosts a variety of exhibits highlighting the town's rich history as one of Iceland's main commercial ports. The museum's turf-roofed stone farm cottage shows how life was lived in the region at the turn of the 20th century. Its reconstructed rooms contain vintage furnishings and artifacts, including cooking equipment and fishing gear.

REYKJANES ART MUSEUM

The **Reykjanes Art Museum** (Tjarnargata 12, Keflavík, tel. 354/421-6700, www.listasafn.reykjanesbaer.is, noon-5pm daily, 1,500ISK) is a charming museum that hosts exhibitions of local artists. The museum gives a taste of the region's eclectic art scene. You can check out contemporary art as well as traditional paintings of the sweeping landscape, from its vast lava fields to the quaint houses along the sea.

REYKJANES MARITIME CENTER

The **Reykjanes Maritime Center** (Duusgata 2, Keflavík, tel. 354/421-6700, noon-5pm daily, 1,500ISK) houses 100 model boats built by a retired local sailor, Grímur Karlsson. Models on display include masted schooners of

Reykjanes Peninsula

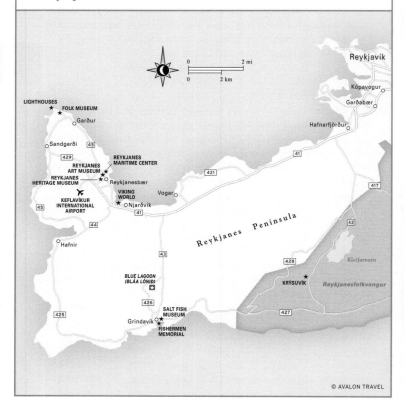

the mid-19th century and steam-powered trawlers of the 20th century. Information is available on the types of boats and when they were used.

ICELANDIC MUSEUM OF ROCK 'N' ROLL

Icelandic Museum of Rock 'n' Roll (Hjallavegur 2, Keflavík, tel. 354/420-1030, www.rokksafn.is, 11am-6pm daily, 1,500ISK) is a perfect stop for those who love the music of Björk, Sigur Rós, Kaleo, and Of Monsters and Men, and are interested in learning about other rock and pop acts from Iceland. Visitors can listen to the music of local artists, see instruments, and check out costumes that have been worn by well-known local musicians, including one of Iceland's biggest pop stars, Páll Óskar. Guests can also learn about the histories of some of the island's most popular bands and singers. Interactive displays include a sound lab where you can have a karaoke-style sing-along or play drums, guitar, or bass. A café and music shop are also on-site.

(Vikingaheimar)

The **Viking World** (Vikingabraut 1, Njarðvík, tel. 354/894-2874, www. vikingaheimar.com, 7am-6pm daily Feb. 1-Oct. 31, 10am-5pm daily Nov. 1-Jan. 31, 1,500ISK) museum is centered on the replica Viking ship *Íslendingur (Icelander),* which was built in 2000 to sail from Iceland to Greenland in commemoration of Leifur Eiríksson's voyage to North America. The ship, which makes for a great photo op, is housed inside a grand building with huge windows overlooking the shore. Lifted several feet from the ground, the ship can be viewed from many angles; tables and chairs below allow you to spend time gazing at the boat with the ocean in the background. A video exhibit shows how Viking ships were constructed. Other exhibitions include information on the settlement of Iceland as well as Norse mythology. When the weather is pleasant, it's great to sit on the large grass field and enjoy a coffee from the café inside. For kids, there's a "settlement zoo" exhibit, which allows children to get up close and personal with baby lambs, calves, and birds.

Sports and Recreation
HORSE RIDING
Extreme Iceland (Skutuvogur 13a, tel. 354/588-1300, www.extremeiceland.is, 19,500ISK) offers a day tour, with 4-5 hours of riding along the Reykjanes Peninsula. Participants explore the vast lava fields by horseback with an experienced guide who takes you along rivers, mountains, even a volcano ridge. The tour is offered year-round and departs from Hafnarfjörður. The tour cost includes all necessary riding equipment.

SWIMMING
The **Vatnaveröld Swimming Pool** (Sunnubraut 31, Keflavík, tel. 354/421-1500, 7am-8pm Mon.-Fri., 8am-6pm Sat.-Sun., 600ISK) in Keflavík is complete with hot tubs, heated pools, and a great swimming area for children. It's a wildly popular spot for locals and gives you a peek into an integral part of Icelandic society.

WHALE-WATCHING
Whale Watching Reykjanes (Reykjanesveg 2, tel. 354/779-8272, www. whalewatchingreykjanes.is, 10,900ISK) runs a tour from Keflavík Harbor. You'll have a chance to see dolphins and an array of whale species including minke, fin, orca, and humpback whales. The tours are three hours and operate on a large, 90-person boat. Tours run year-round and leave once a day at 1pm.

Food
Café Duus (Duusgata 10, Keflavík, tel. 354/421-7080, www.duus.is, entrées from 2,000ISK) is a lovely café based in the Duus Museum, Reykjanesbær's arts and culture center. It has a casual atmosphere and attracts both locals

and tourists. An impressive menu features creamy lobster soup, a popular starter, and main courses like pan-fried lobster, tandoori chicken, and vegetarian curry. The restaurant features spectacular harbor views and the quality of food keeps people coming back.

Housed in the Hótel Keflavík, **KEF Restaurant & Bar** (Vatnsnesvegur, Keflavík, tel. 354/420-7000, www.kef.is, 5am-10am and 6pm-9:30pm daily, entrées from 3,500ISK) is known for serving classic fish and meat dishes. Expect to see Icelandic cod, salmon, and lamb recipes on the menu. The chef focuses on sourcing local ingredients whenever possible. It opens for breakfast at 5am for early birds. During the winter, if the northern lights decide to make an appearance, the restaurant's glass façade allows expansive views of the lights dancing and flickering in the deep black sky.

Situated in the heart of the town, **Langbest** (Keilisbraut 771, Keflavík, tel. 354/421-4777, www.langbest.is, 11:30am-9:30pm daily, entrées from 1,600ISK) serves up pizza, sandwiches, and fish-and-chips. It's a great place to stop for something quick and affordable.

Accommodations

At **Hótel Berg** (Bakkavegur 17, Keflavík, tel. 354/422-7922, www.hotelberg.is, rooms from 30,000ISK), modernized rooms are comfortable and have flat-screen televisions and free Wi-Fi. If you get one of the two loft suites during the winter months, you might catch a glimpse of the northern lights from the skylight.

Rooms at **Hótel Keflavík** (Vatnsvegur 12, Keflavík, tel. 354/420-7000, www.kef.is, rooms from 34,000ISK) are a bit small, but each room has a private bathroom, comfortable bed, and sweeping views of the lava fields. Staff is warm and helpful, and an in-house restaurant serves traditional Icelandic fare as well as some international favorites.

Keflavík's centrally located **Hótel Keilir** (Hafnargata 37, Keflavík, tel. 354/420-9800, www.eng.hotelkelir.is, rooms from 24,000ISK), boasts modern, minimalist decor, average-sized rooms, and small bathrooms. A family suite is available that can comfortably sleep five people. This hotel is a good budget option and just a five-minute drive from the airport.

Start Hostel (Lindarbraut 637, tel. 354/420-6050, www.starthostel.is, rooms from 16,000ISK) offers a mix of doubles, quadruples, family rooms, and dorm beds. The rooms are clean but bare bones, with just beds and a small table. Some rooms have private bathrooms, others share facilities, and there is a common room with a kitchen, luggage storage, free parking, and free Wi-Fi. Guests have access to laundry machines and Keflavík International Airport is just an eight-minute drive away.

Information and Services

Reykjanesbær's **tourist office** (Hafnargata 36, tel. 354/421-5660, www.visitreykjanes.is, 1pm-6pm daily) offers a booking service for tours and has brochures on activities, restaurants, and sights in the region.

Reykjanesbær is 49 kilometers southwest from Reykjavík. By car, take Route 41, which is paved, to reach the region. It's about a 50-minute drive.

The **Fly Bus** (tel. 354/580-5400, www.flybus.is) runs regularly from **Keflavík International Airport** to the BSÍ bus station in Reykjavík, from where you can get a shuttle to your downtown hotel. It takes about 50 minutes to get from Keflavík to BSÍ bus station, and buses depart about 40 minutes after flights land. One-way tickets cost 2,500ISK.

If you are staying in Reykjanesbær, be sure to contact your hotel or guesthouse to see if there is a shuttle to pick you up at the airport. If not, taxis are available at the airport.

There are tours for sights in Reykjanesbær, but if you want the freedom to roam, renting a car is essential.

GARÐUR

Garður is a placid seaside town on the northwest tip of Reykjanes and a great place to spend a couple of hours. Garður is best known for a pair of lighthouses. On sunny summer days, locals and tourists picnic by the lighthouses, basking in the sun and enjoying the serenity and scenery. The lighthouses are a great spot to catch a glimpse of the northern lights in the winter, as the location is away from the bright lights of downtown.

Sights
LIGHTHOUSES

The highlight of Garður is the two lighthouses, each with unique charm. The older, more traditional red-striped lighthouse was built in 1847, and the newer square-designed one was built in 1944 in a more modern Nordic style. This is a popular destination for photos. Fishing boats can often be seen from shore, and there is rich birdlife in the region, ranging from hordes of gulls circling in the summer months to ravens dominating the skies in the winter. It's also common to see arctic terns and gannets in the summer. In the winter, the lighthouses appear against a backdrop of mist and mystery, and if you're lucky, you will see northern lights dancing in the night sky.

FOLK MUSEUM
(Byggðasafn Garðskaga)

The **Folk Museum** (Skagabraut 100, tel. 354/422-7220, www.svgardur.is, 1pm-5pm daily Apr. 1-Oct. 31, open by appointment the rest of the year, free) sits amid a rugged landscape with thriving birdlife. The quaint museum houses items that were essential for the livelihood of residents on both land and sea, including tools, fishing items, and maps. It offers a window into what life was like in past generations, reminding visitors that life in Iceland was not easy for early settlers. The museum also has an extensive collection of 60 functional engines provided by local resident Guðni Ingimundarson.

Food and Accommodations

The Old Lighthouse Café (Garðskagi, tel. 354/422-7220, 11:30am-8:30pm daily May-Oct., entrées from 1,800ISK), housed in an actual lighthouse, offers cakes, coffee, soft drinks, and light meals. It's a good place to grab a quick bite, and you can also go to the top of the lighthouse for a great view of the Reykjanes Peninsula, the lava fields, and if you're lucky, maybe a whale in the distance.

Guesthouse Garður (Skagabraut 46, tel. 354/660-7894, www.guesthousegardur.is, apartments from 26,000ISK) is a charming guesthouse with seven apartments ranging from studios to two-bedrooms available year-round. Located close to the harbor, the apartments have private kitchens, bathrooms with showers, free Wi-Fi, and satellite TV. The friendly staff can help arrange local tours, including golfing, bird-watching, and fishing. The cozy guesthouse is just a 10-minute drive to Keflavík airport.

CAMPING

The **Garðskagi campground** (Skagabraut, tel. 354/422-7220, 1,200ISK) is close to the two lighthouses in a quiet stretch of town. Campers have access to running water and toilets year-round.

Transportation

Garður is 55 kilometers west of Reykjavík. By car, take Route 41 to Route 45.

ELDEY ISLAND

Situated about 15 kilometers southwest from the southernmost tip of the Reykjanes Peninsula, Eldey Island is made up of sheer cliffs that jut out of the ocean and reach 77 meters high. Birdlife thrives on the island; Eldey has one of the biggest gannet bird colonies in the world. In recent years, an estimated 70,000 gannets have bred on the island from June to August. The best view of the island is from the Reykjanes Lighthouse; the GPS coordinates are N 63.8151, W 22.7033.

GRINDAVÍK

Grindavík is a placid fishing town steeped in fish trade history. Many of the same families have been trolling these waters for generations, and visitors can see fishers hauling their daily bounty of cod out of the harbor by day and dine on the local catch at night. The Grindavík area's greatest claim to fame, however, is the giant man-made geothermal expanse of the Blue Lagoon.

Sights
★ BLUE LAGOON
(Bláa Lónið)

Built on an 800-year old lava field, the **Blue Lagoon** (Svartsengi, tel. 354/420-8800, www.bluelagoon.com, 8am-10pm daily Jan.1-May 25 and Aug. 21-Oct. 1, 7am-11pm daily May 26-June 29, 7am-midnight daily June

30-Aug. 20, 8am-8pm daily Oct. 2-Dec. 31) covers an area of 8,700 square meters and draws visitors from around the world to soak in its gloriously milky-blue waters amid a dreamlike atmosphere. The heated water, which ranges 37-39°C (98-102°F), is heavenly any time of year. Enjoying the steamy air while soaking during the summer is lovely, especially on sunny days. And in the winter, a visit here is eerie and wonderful; watching as snow falls from the jet-black December sky or as northern lights dance across it while lounging in the hot water is sublime.

The water isn't deep, less than five feet, and the bottom is covered with white silica mud, the result of a natural process of recondensation. It's common to see visitors cover their faces with the mud—it's great for your skin, and all guests receive a free silica mud mask with standard admission. The gift shop sells Blue Lagoon skin products that have ingredients ranging from silica mud to algae found in other parts of Iceland. At the Lagoon Bar, a swim-up bar in the main section of the lagoon, you can purchase drinks to be enjoyed while lounging in the waters. There are also two steam baths on the property, as well as a dry sauna and massage area, and spa treatments are available.

The standard entrance fee is 6,100ISK for those over 14 years of age, 3,400ISK for disabled visitors, and free for children 2-13. Children under the age of 2 are not allowed at the lagoon. You can also upgrade your ticket to include add-ons like an algae mask, your first drink of choice, and a towel to use, but towels, swimsuits, robes, and slippers can also be rented à la carte. Because of the increase in tourism over the past few years, the Blue Lagoon now requires you to book a time slot ahead of your arrival, which you can do on its website. Reserve your time at least several weeks before your trip. Thousands of people visit the site every day, and it can get quite crowded during summer months. For the best chance of avoiding crowds, try to book early in the morning or late in the evening.

Many tours feature a visit to the Blue Lagoon, but if you're traveling

the Blue Lagoon

independently, it makes sense to visit right after you fly in or before you head home, as it's very close to Keflavík airport. A rejuvenating soak is a great way to kick off your trip or end it on a relaxing note.

Driving from Reykjavík, the Blue Lagoon is about 48 kilometers, roughly 45 minutes, away on paved roads; head southwest on Route 41 and turn left onto Route 43. From Keflavík International Airport, the Blue Lagoon is about 23 kilometers away; take Route 41 and turn right onto Route 43, and you'll arrive in approximately 20 minutes. If you're making your way to or from the airport, note that the Blue Lagoon offers luggage storage. Bus transfers via **Reykjavík Excursions** (tel. 354/580-5400, www.re.is) can be booked in conjunction with Blue Lagoon entrance tickets; the buses run between both Reykjavík and the Blue Lagoon and Keflavík International Airport and the Blue Lagoon. Buses are available from Reykjavík to the Blue Lagoon, every hour 7am-7pm year-round, with additional services seasonally. From KEF to the Blue Lagoon, there are seven daily departures year-round and added service during the high season.

SALTFISH MUSEUM
(Saltfisksetur)

The **Saltfish Museum** (Hafnargata 12A, tel. 354/420-1190, 9am-6pm daily, entrance 1,200ISK) tells the story of Iceland's fish trade from 1770 to 1965, the period when saltfish was Iceland's top export. Photos, fishing equipment, and even a full-size fishing boat from the early 20th century are on display, explaining the economic and cultural importance of saltfish to Iceland. If you're curious about the region, would like to learn more about processing saltfish in the olden days, or would like to get a look at an old-school fishing boat, be sure to stop by.

FISHERMEN MEMORIAL

A sad part of Iceland's fishing history is the stories of men who went out to sea to never return. There's a moving memorial in downtown Grindavík, in the main garden near the Saltfish Museum, showing a mother with her son and daughter waiting for their fisherman husband/father to return home from sea. It's a reminder that the fish used for consumption and trade has come at a high price for many families over the years. The memorial was created by sculptor Ragnar Kjartansson.

Sports and Recreation
ATV RIDING

For those looking for a little adventure, **4x4 Adventures Iceland** (Tangasund 1, Grindavík, tel. 354/857-3001, www.4x4adventuresiceland. is, 13,900ISK) offers a number of ATV/quad bike tours that let you get off the beaten track. Its one-hour Panorama tour takes travelers around the Reykjanes Peninsula and near rocky lava formations, mountains, and even to a view over the Blue Lagoon. No experience is necessary for this year-round tour.

The **Grindavík Swimming Pool** (Austurvegi 1, tel. 354/426-7555, www.
grindavik.is, 7am-8pm Mon.-Fri., 10am-5pm Sat.-Sun. June-Aug., 500ISK)
is one of the best pools in South Iceland with its 25-meter pool, hot tubs,
tanning beds, waterslide, children's pool, and fitness center.

GOLF

Just four kilometers southwest from the Blue Lagoon, **Húsatóftir Golf
Course** (Húsatóftum, tel. 354/426-8720, paller@grindavik.is, greens fees
Mon.-Fri. 3,000ISK, Sat.-Sun. 3,500ISK) is an 18-hole facility where visitors
can golf late May-early September, depending on the weather. The scenic
course offers picturesque views. It can be busy with locals during the high
season of June-July, so be sure to call ahead for a tee time.

Food

Hja Hollu (Víkurbraut 62, tel. 354/896-5316, www.hjahollu.is, 8am-5pm
Mon.-Fri., 11am-5pm Sat., entrées from 1,890ISK) is modern and casual
with a friendly atmosphere and menu chock-full of healthy options like
salads and vegan dishes. Guests can also choose from soups, sandwiches,
pizzas, and wraps.

The ★ **Lava Blue Lagoon Restaurant** (Svartsengi, tel. 354/420-8800,
www.bluelagoon.com, 11:30am-9pm daily, entrées from 5,900ISK) is very
much a spa restaurant: ingredients are local, and the recipes are healthy.
You will find fresh vegetables and fish as well as lean meats. The menu accommodates a host of dietary requirements. The atmosphere is minimalist chic with cool hues and modern accents. Casual clothing is allowed.

★ **Salthúsið** (Stamphólsvegur 9, tel. 354/426-9700, www.salthusid.is,
noon-10pm daily mid-May-mid-Sept., noon-9pm mid-Sept.-mid-May, entrées from 3,300ISK), or "the Salt House," is a favorite among local fishers,
residents, and tourists. A lot of saltfish is on the quiet eatery's menu, but
guests can also choose from lamb and chicken dishes, as well as burgers,
sandwiches, and fish-and-chips. The garlic-roasted lobster with salad and
garlic bread is delicious. If you have room, be sure to check out the decadent
dessert menu, which includes items such as deep-fried bananas with vanilla
ice cream and caramel sauce, and French chocolate cake with fresh cream.

Max's Restaurant (Grindavíkurvegi 1, tel. 354/426-8650, www.nli.is,
entrées from 3,200ISK) is the in-house restaurant at the Northern Light
Inn. The atmosphere is very much that of a hotel restaurant, with good service and not many surprises, but it charms with huge windows overlooking
mountains and lava fields. The menu consists of classic Icelandic food like
lamb fillet and fresh fish dishes.

Accommodations

The ★ **Blue Lagoon Silica Hotel** (Svartsengi, tel. 354/420-8806, www.
bluelagoon.com/Clinic, doubles from 46,000ISK) is a luxurious hotel connected to the Blue Lagoon. It has 35 bright and airy double rooms, each with

private bathrooms and a terrace overlooking the surrounding lava fields. Silica offers luxury beds, modern decor, and beautiful views of the lagoon. Guests have access to a private lagoon open daily 9am-10pm.

Geo Hotel Grindavík (Víkurbraut 58, tel. 354/421-4000, www.geohotel. is, rooms from 22,000ISK) has double and family rooms, all with private bathroom facilities. The hotel's design includes a spacious social area for guests to relax in cozy surroundings. Room walls are painted in muted colors, and there are wood floors and minimalist furniture. Shops and conveniences are nearby in the town center.

Open year-round, **Guesthouse Borg** (Boragarhraun 2, tel. 354/895-8686, www.guesthouseborg.com, rooms from 15,000ISK) is a basic, no-frills guesthouse in the center of Grindavík and the best budget-friendly option in the area. The seven-room guesthouse has shared kitchen facilities, bathrooms, and washing machines, and is a five-minute drive from the Blue Lagoon. It's a clean and comfortable place to stay, but nothing to write home about.

The 32-room guesthouse **Northern Light Inn** (Grindavíkurvegi 1, tel. 354/426-8650, www.nli.is, doubles from 36,000ISK) offers cozy, bright, rooms with free Wi-Fi, satellite TV, and sweeping views. An in-house restaurant serves classic Icelandic fare with plenty of fish and lamb dishes, as well as a couple of vegetarian options. Its proximity to the Blue Lagoon is a big draw for tourists: It's just a 0.7-kilometer walk from the lagoon.

CAMPING

You can camp from mid-May to mid-September at the popular **Grindavík's Campsite** (Austurvegur 26, tel. 354/660-7323, 1,390ISK) by the harbor. It accommodates tents, RVs, and campers, with access to hookups (electricity costs an extra 1,000ISK per night) and a dump station. There's a paved entrance and a large parking area, and the grassy field has beautiful mountain views. The campsite offers laundry facilities, a common eating area, and a playground with swings and a spider net.

Information and Services

The tourist information center is located in the **Saltfish Museum** (Hafnargata 12A, tel. 354/420-1190, 10am-5pm daily). The gas station N1 and grocery chain Netto are situated downtown on Víkurbraut.

Transportation

By car, Grindavík is 50 kilometers from Reykjavík. Drivers should take Route 41 west to Route 43 south, both paved roads. It's about a 50-minute drive.

There are three daily departures from BSÍ bus station (www.bsi.is) in Reykjavík to Grindavík, offered year-round through **Reykjavík Excursions** (tel. 354/580-5400, www.re.is, 4,500ISK). There are return buses to Reykjavík as well. The buses go to both the Blue Lagoon and the center of Grindavík (about 1.25 hours).

The Krýsuvík geothermal area, which is 35 kilometers south of Reykjavík, is popular among geology buffs and hikers. Gurgling mud pools bubble from the yellow, red, and orange clay-like earth, intertwined with dancing steam and hot springs. The many hiking paths allow you to feel lost in the outer space-like atmosphere. The region gives you a great sense of Iceland's raw, natural geothermal energy, which powers much of the island. Take some time to roam, but be sure to stay within the designated roped-off areas to avoid getting burned by spray and steam. To get to the region, take Route 42 south from Reykjavík. It's about a 40-minute drive on the paved road.

The Golden Circle

If you ask an Icelander which tour you should take if you want a taste of Iceland outside of Reykjavík, he or she will most likely recommend the Golden Circle. Encompassing the three most visited sights in South Iceland, the Golden Circle gives you a slice of Icelandic history at Þingvellir, a view of Iceland's bubbling geothermal activity at Geysir, and a peek at a roaring, powerful waterfall at Gullfoss. The sights are classically Icelandic, and are postcard perfect in summer or winter.

Because of the popularity of the sights, it's pretty easy to get there. You can prebook a tour through many tourism companies, or simply go to Reykjavík's main bus terminal, **BSÍ** (Vatnsmýrarvegur 10, Reykjavík, tel. 354/562-1011, www.bsi.is), and buy a same-day ticket through **Reykjavík Excursions** (tel. 354/580-5400, www.re.is) for 10,900ISK for an eight-hour tour. If you have a rental car and want to view the sights independently, take Route 1 to Route 36 for Þingvellir. Continue on Route 36 then Routes 365, 37, and 35 to Geysir. From Geysir continue on Route 35 to Gullfoss, before looping back toward Reykjavík heading southwest on Routes 35 and 1. In total, the Golden Circle is an approximately 300-kilometer paved circular route, leaving from and returning to Reykjavík.

ÞINGVELLIR NATIONAL PARK

The birth of Iceland as a nation happened at Þingvellir. Literally translated to "Parliament Plains," Þingvellir was the site of Iceland's first general assembly, which was said to have been established in the year 930, and was the meeting place of the Icelandic parliament until 1798. Many significant sights are at Þingvellir, including Almannagjá and Law Rock (Lögberg). Þingvellir was established as a national park in 1930.

Visitors also come to the area for its geological significance, as it is the site of a rift valley that marks the crest of the **Mid-Atlantic Ridge**. It's also home to Þingvallavatn, the largest natural lake on the island, which has a surface area of 84 square kilometers. Visiting the park itself is free, but there's a parking fee (500ISK).

The Golden Circle

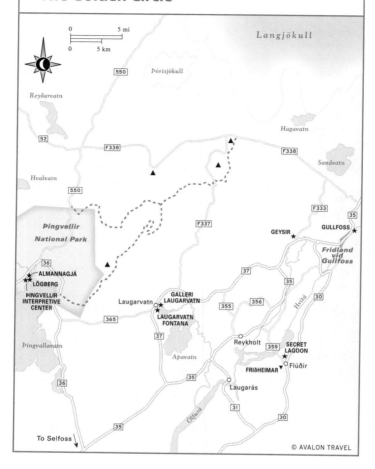

© AVALON TRAVEL

Sights

ÞINGVELLIR INTERPRETIVE CENTER

The Þingvellir Interpretive Center (tel. 354/482-2660, www.thingvel-lir.is, 9am-8pm daily June-Aug., 9am-5pm Sept.-Apr., free) gives a great overview of the national park, its history, and its geological significance. Stop in to see the interactive display and then pick up hiking maps at the information center next door.

ALMANNAGJÁ

The park's stony, moss-covered landscape is home to Almannagjá (All Man's Gorge), which is the tallest cliff face in the national park and the original backdrop to the Alþing. This rock structure is considered the edge of the North American plate, which visitors can view up close. It's an impressive sight, so be sure you have your camera ready.

LÖGBERG
Lögberg (Law Rock) is where Icelandic democracy began. Iceland's Commonwealth period ran from 930 till 1262, and during that time, the Law Rock was the center of the Alþing (parliament). Members of the Alþing gave speeches and held events at the rock, including confirming of the year's calendar and issuing legal rulings. A man known as the "law speaker," who was responsible for understanding all laws and required to memorize them, read the procedural laws aloud every summer, standing on the rock.

ÖXARÁ RIVER
The Öxará (Axe) River flows over seemingly endless lava fields, emitting a haunting mist in the winter months. It's serene and eerie until it reaches Öxaráfoss, where the water tumbles and roars over the cliffs. At the river's edge are a church and farmhouse, the latter of which is the official summer residence of Iceland's prime minister. The church, Þingvallakirkja (9am-5pm daily mid-May-early Sept., free), is a charming wood structure built in traditional Icelandic design that dates from 1859. Visitors can go inside, take photos, and sit on a pew and reflect. The interior features a wooden pulpit and bells from earlier churches. There's a small cemetery behind the church where celebrated poets Einar Benediktsson and Jonasa Hallgrimsson are buried.

Sports and Recreation
DIVING AND SNORKELING
Scuba diving or snorkeling in the naturally filtered, pure water of Þingvallavatn lake is sublime. Surveying the underwater basalt walls,

Þingvellir National Park

multicolored algae, and sloping sands is magical and unique—you're able to snorkel or scuba in the Silfa fissure, the enormous crack between the Eurasian and North American continental plates. Don't even think about going in without a drysuit, as the water temperature hovers around 3°C (37°F). Diving is possible year-round. There are rules to obey, so don't attempt to go without a guide. **Dive Iceland** (Ásbúðartröð 17, Hafnarfjörður, tel. 354/699-3000, www.dive.is) offers a two-tank dive package for about 44,990ISK. Travelers must be dry-suit certified to dive. Snorkeling tours start at 19,990ISK.

FISHING

Boats are not allowed on the lake, but fishing permits are sold at the information center. Tourists have a chance of catching arctic char and brown trout. Be sure to obey the rules and pay for the permit. The fishing season at the lake runs May 1-September 15, and permits are about 40,000ISK.

HIKING

Þingvellir is lovely for the casual hiker. Acres of flat lava fields make it an easy hiking spot, but be sure to be careful of open rock fissures along the way; you could fall in. There are scores of foot trails and plenty of interesting rock formations and rugged terrain to see. You can get information about trails and the surrounding area at the visitors center. If you're looking to scale some small mountains, check out **Mount Syðstasúla** (1,085 meters), which is in the northern region of the park and is the park's easiest peak to climb. The view from the top is spectacular. The moderate hike is 13 kilometers round-trip and takes about seven hours.

HORSE RIDING

Þingvellir is a popular spot for riding horses, with several trails that offer the chance to check out some of the more beautiful and geologically significant areas of the park. Seeing the region by horseback is a beautiful way to survey the land. **Reykjavík Excursions** (tel. 354/580-5400, www.re.is) offers a year-round horse-riding day tour in Þingvellir for 23,300ISK.

Food and Accommodations

There are no hotels within Þingvellir National Park. However, there are accommodations in nearby Laugarvatn and Selfoss. If you would like to stay within the park limits, your only option is **camping** at one of Þingvellir's five campgrounds, spread across two areas of the park: the Leirar section, which is a five-minute walk from the Þingvellir information center, and the Vatnskot section, which is by Lake Þingvallavatn. The Leirar campground is divided into four campsites: Fagrabrekka, Syðri-Leirar, Hvannabrekka, and Nyrðri-Leirar. The Vatnskot campground is situated at an abandoned farm by the lake. All campsites have access to toilets, electricity, and cooking facilities. The difference in the two sections is not about amenities, but whether you want to camp close to the lake or views and spacious fields. The campgrounds are open June 1-September 30, and cost 1,300ISK per person.

Information and Services

The **tourist information center** (tel. 354/482-2660, www.thingvellir.is, 9am-8pm daily June 1-Aug. 31, 9am-6pm daily Sept. 1-May 31) is close to the car park. Be advised that there is a service fee of 200ISK to use the bathroom.

Transportation

Þingvellir is 46 kilometers northeast of Reykjavík. By car, take Route 1 to Route 36, which will take you to the northern part of the park.

While there is no public transportation available to get to the park, a number of tours include a stop at Þingvellir. Check out **Reykjavík Excursions** (tel. 354/580-5400, www.re.is) for daily departures.

LAUGARVATN

Laugarvatn, or "Bathing Waters," is a lake situated between Þingvellir and the geothermal hot spot of Geysir. Historically, members of Iceland's parliament (Alþing) visited the springs due to their proximity to where parliament met at Þingvellir for hundreds of years. The lake's water temperature hovers around 104°F, making it a unique and warm swimming experience.

Sights

GALLERI LAUGARVATN

When not enjoying the soothing hot springs or the vistas, steal away for a few minutes at **Galleri Laugarvatn** (Haholt 1, tel. 354/486-1016, www.gallerilaugarvatn.is, 1pm-5pm daily), a charming little gallery that features local handicrafts, ranging from glass tea light holders to unique paper crafts.

LAUGARVATN FONTANA

The **Laugarvatn Fontana** (Hverabraut 1, tel. 354/486-1400, www.fontana.is, 10am-11pm daily June 9-Aug. 20, 11am-10pm daily Aug. 21-June 8, 4,200ISK adults, 2,200ISK children 13-16, free for children 12 and under) is worth a stop before or after you visit Geysir. The facility's sauna captures the steam just as it escapes from the earth. You can bask in the natural sauna and hot springs, enjoying the geothermal energy up close and personal. Towels, bathing suits, and bathrobes can be rented at the spa.

For an experience unique to the region, each day at 2:30pm there is a walk from the reception area to the on-site geothermal bakery. Visitors can watch as the staff digs out rye bread that's been buried in the ground, left to bake naturally in the geothermally heated earth. You can try the bread, served hot from the ground with some butter—it's delicious!

SWIMMING

Situated downtown, the **Laugarvatn Swimming Pool** (Hverabraut 2, tel. 354/486-1251, 10am-10pm Mon.-Fri., 10am-6pm Sat.-Sun. June-mid-Aug., 5pm-8pm Mon., Wed., and Fri., 1pm-5pm Sat. mid-Aug.-May, 600ISK) is popular among locals, and it's a nice break from the summer tourist rush at the Fontana spa nearby. Head here if you would like a quiet spot to take a dip.

Food

At **Restaurant Linden** (Lindarbraut 2, tel. 354/486-1262, www.laugarvatn. is, noon-10pm daily, entrées from 3,600ISK), owner and head chef Baldur Öxdal Halldórsson has created an upscale, fine-dining experience in a town with fewer than 300 residents. Guests have a lot of choices, from Icelandic mainstays to more exotic fare, with dishes ranging from reindeer meat burgers and pan-fried arctic char to tender lamb fillets and smoked cod. The classic decor and friendly staff make this little restaurant a treasure.

Accommodations

Location is key for **Hótel Edda ML Laugarvatn** (Skólatún, tel. 354/444-4810, www.hoteledda.is, mid-June-mid-Aug., rooms from 11,500ISK), as this 101-room hotel is a popular stop for those touring the Golden Circle. Rooms are basic and no-frills, with double beds, IKEA-style furniture, and crisp white bedding. Thirty-two rooms have private bathrooms, while the rest share facilities, and there is free Wi-Fi in common areas. Guests get a 10 percent discount for the geothermal steam baths at the nearby Fontana spa.

Efstidalur II (Bláskógabyggð, tel. 354/486-1186, www.efstidalur.is, rooms from 25,000ISK) is a charming farmhouse bed-and-breakfast with an in-house restaurant, friendly staff, and horse rentals. Situated close to the Fontana spa, the B&B is also in the proximity of the Golden Circle.

Golden Circle Apartments (Laugarbraut, tel. 354/487-1212, www.goldencircleapartments.is, apartments from 19,000ISK) offers 25 apartments that are modern and perfect for families, with fully equipped kitchens, private bathrooms, a TV, free Wi-Fi, and free parking. Apartments are spacious, have new appliances, and are close to town attractions.

One of the busiest hostels in South Iceland, **Laugarvatn Youth Hostel** (Dalsel, tel. 354/486-1215, www.laugarvatnhostel.is, open all year, double rooms from 10,900ISK) can accommodate 140 people in single, double, and family rooms. Ten rooms have private bathroom facilities, while the rest share. Kitchen and laundry facilities are available, and the staff is very warm and helpful. There's also a big hot tub on the property.

Transportation

Laugarvatn is just 77 kilometers northeast from Reykjavík and is easily accessible by car and bus. If driving from Þingvellir, take Routes 36 and 365 to Route 37.

The **Strætó** bus company (tel. 354/540-2700, www.straeto.is) has one daily departure to Laugarvatn year-round, leaving from the Mjodd bus terminal (tel. 354/587-0230) in Reykjavík. The trip is about 2.5 hours, and it costs 2,520ISK.

GEYSIR

Iceland's geysers are the most obvious demonstration of the island's natural geothermal energy, and historically, Geysir is the country's most famous example of the phenomenon—it's actually the source of the word "geyser." Geologists theorized that in the 13th century earthquakes stirred the underground workings of the natural hot springs here, causing them to gush, releasing pressure, steam, and water up to 20 meters into the air.

Visitors to the site today aren't going to see the dormant Geysir erupt—it hasn't blown since 2005. But don't fret, because Geysir's nearby cousin, **Strokkur** (Churn), erupts every seven minutes or so. Crowds gather to watch the frequent eruptions, and the churning, gurgling pool of hot water turning out a rush of pressure from the clay-like earth is an impressive sight; be sure to have your camera ready. Please be careful and stay behind the ropes or you may get hit with hot spray.

After walking around the geothermal area, stop at the **visitors center** (9am-10pm daily). It has a short multimedia exhibition about the geology of the region, a small café serving refreshments, and a souvenir shop.

Food and Accommodations

You can't stay any closer to the geysers than at the **Hótel Geysir** (Geysir, tel. 354/480-6800, www.geysircenter.is, rooms from 23,000ISK). The property features posh suites that have huge Jacuzzi tubs and luxurious beds in a location just two minutes from the geysers. Guests can also stay in chalets on the property that are essentially double rooms. The decor is a bit rustic, but the rooms are comfortable. Visitors have access to an outdoor swimming

the Strokkur geyser erupting

pool and hot tub. The in-house **restaurant** (8am-10pm daily) serves up delicious dishes ranging from fresh Icelandic cod to lamb and beef entrées. A lunch buffet is popular among tourists. A three-course dinner menu will run you about 8,000ISK.

CAMPING

About 100 meters from the Geysir area is a **campground** (tel. 354/480-6800, 1,700ISK) that has hot showers, pool access, and a common barbecue area. Hótel Geysir operates the campsite, and you pay at the Geysir Shops just across from the campground. For an additional 1,000ISK you can have access to electricity, and the use of the swimming pool and hot tub at Hótel Geysir will run you an additional 500ISK.

Transportation

Geysir is about a 1.5-hour drive east from Reykjavík. You start out on Route 1 and then take Route 35, which takes you directly to the site.

If following the Golden Circle route, continue from Laugarvatn on Route 37 to Route 35 for Geysir.

GULLFOSS

The thundering, roaring waterfall of Gullfoss epitomizes the raw beauty of Iceland. Gullfoss (Golden Falls) tumbles into the Hvíta (White) River, which is a perfect name given the turbulent white water. There are three levels of water at the falls, ranging from 11 to 21 meters, meeting at a 70-meter gorge. If you get too close, expect to get soaked.

Because of Iceland's changing weather, you have a good chance to see a rainbow over the falls, making for a perfect snapshot of your visit. Plan to walk around the site, enjoying not only the wonder of the falls, but also the beautiful surrounding landscape. In the summer, there are miles of

Gullfoss

The Secret Lagoon

The **Secret Lagoon (Gamla Laugin)** (Hvammsvegur, tel. 354/555-3351, www.secretlagoon.is, 10am-10pm May 1-Sept. 30, 11am-8pm Oct. 1-Apr. 30, 2,800ISK adults, free for children 14 and under) has become a popular alternative (and cheaper at that) to the Blue Lagoon. It's located in Fluðir, a blip of a village with not much going on, but the Secret Lagoon brings tourists by the thousands while still offering a slightly more intimate, less touristy experience than the Blue Lagoon. The surroundings here are beautiful, with farmland and a geothermal area lush with moss covering lava stones and natural springs bubbling and steaming, just past the water's edge. You can rent towels and swimsuits here, and there is a café with drinks and snacks for sale.

If following the conventional Golden Circle route from Gulfoss down Route 35 back to Route 1, you'll bypass the Secret Lagoon. But if you make a slightly larger circle, jumping off Route 35 and taking Route 30 south instead, you'll pass right by Fluðir; it's about 38 kilometers south of Gulfoss, a 30-minute drive, and afterward you can connect from Route 30 back to Route 1 and Reykjavík.

lush green grass and frequent rainbows on sunny/rainy days. Be careful; it could be slippery.

No matter what time of year, there are scores of tour buses and independent drivers visiting the falls, and that's for a very good reason: It's gorgeous.

There is an ongoing fight between landowners and the Icelandic government over whether to charge visitors a fee to visit the falls. As of summer 2017, it was undecided and still in the courts.

An on-site café includes a souvenir shop and offers some brochures about the surrounding area.

Food and Accommodations

A short walk from the falls and parking area, **Gullfoss Café (Gullfosskaffi)** (tel. 354/486-6500, www.gullfoss.is, 9am-9:30pm daily, entrées from 1,800ISK) is the place to go when you're in the area. The Icelandic lamb meat soup on the menu is a winner, and a favorite among visitors, but sandwiches, cakes, and coffee are also available.

Hótel Gullfoss (Brattholt, tel. 354/486-8979, www.hotelgullfoss.is, rooms from 27,000ISK) is situated perfectly, just three kilometers from the falls in a remote area. The resort-like atmosphere is comfortable and a great place to spend the night while touring the Golden Circle. Every room has a private bathroom and is classically furnished with comfortable beds. An in-house restaurant and hot tub out back make for a comfortable stay.

On Route 35 between Gullfoss and Selfoss, you might stop for lunch at ★ **Friðheimar** (Bláskógabyggð, tel. 354/486-8894, www.fridheimar.is, noon-4pm daily), located in Reykholt about a half hour and 30 kilometers south of Gullfoss. The farm is home to tomato greenhouses and a restaurant, as well as a horse-breeding operation. It's an ideal place to have lunch: Tomatoes don't get any fresher in Iceland, and the menu takes advantage of this with items like tomato soup and creative Bloody Marys. Call ahead for lunch reservations. Groups of 10 or more can take a tour of the greenhouse with the owner or a staff member. Tours are offered year-round; email fridheimar@fridheimar.is for more information.

Transportation

By car, Gullfoss is 115 kilometers northeast from Reykjavík. The drive takes about 1.5 hours on Routes 1 and 35.

Gullfoss is about 10 kilometers from Geysir on Route 35.

Background

The Landscape

GEOGRAPHY

Iceland is the westernmost European country, situated in the North Atlantic between North America and Europe. Iceland is east of Greenland and south of the Arctic Circle, atop the northern Mid-Atlantic Ridge. It lies 859 kilometers from Scotland and 4,200 kilometers from New York City. The area of Iceland is 103,022 square kilometers, and a frequent comparison among Icelandic tour guides is that Iceland is roughly the size of the U.S. state Kentucky.

Climate

Iceland isn't as cold as you may think. The Gulf Stream swirls along the western and southern coasts and works to moderate Iceland's climate. But "moderate" doesn't mean "calm," as the Gulf Stream is responsible for the frequent weather changes—as in lots of wind and rain. The biggest climate challenge is the unpredictability of it. The "summer" tourist season runs from the end of May to the beginning of September, and during that time, the climate ranges from rainy May days to the midnight sun in July to the possibility of snow in September. The winter climate brings colder temperatures, dark days, whipping winds, and the possibility of seeing northern lights flicker and dance on clear nights.

Weather

Weather in Iceland is not casual conversation, but serious business. Weather forecasts are frequent but largely hit or miss. The weather can change rapidly, from calm winds and sunny skies to rain, snow, sleet and back to calm wind and sunny skies, all in the same hour. It's unpredictable, frustrating, exhilarating, and confusing for many tourists, but Icelanders have learned to adapt and go with the flow. As a result, plans tend to be loose, whether it's for meeting friends for coffee or a going for a job interview. If the weather acts up, locals understand.

Some of the most extreme weather you could experience on this island is wind—the type of wind in winter that could knock you off your feet. If the weather forecast is showing strong winds, especially in the countryside, alter your plans accordingly. Do not underestimate the wind, and be sure to heed any storm advisories. Be safe, smart, and prepared. The changing conditions are part of the experience of traveling to Iceland, and the key is being prepared with layers of clothing, proper footwear, and waterproof outerwear.

Previous: Eyjafjallajökull eruption in 2010; the northern lights.

Geology

Iceland is a volcanic island constantly in flux, with magma breaking through fissures and periodic eruptions that redesign the rocky landscape. Iceland's land is made up of igneous rock, most of which is basalt, which forms from cooling magma. Most of Iceland's mountains were formed with basalt that has been carved by water and ice erosion. Earthquakes are a common occurrence, but large tremors are rarely felt.

VOLCANOES

Volcanic eruptions are a growing source of tourism for the country. Local travel companies offer helicopter, jeep, and airplane tours when an eruption occurs. Most of Iceland's volcanic eruptions, such as the 2014-2015 Holuhraun eruption, are fissure vents, where lava seeps out of the cracks in the earth's crust. Holuhraun produced fountains of lava shooting out of the earth, delighting photographers and keeping volcanologists busy trying to determine if the nearby Bárðarbunga volcano would erupt. The three most active volcanoes on the island are Katla, Hekla, and Eyjafjallajökull. Eyjafjallajökull erupted in 2010, grounding air travel in Europe for days thanks to a large ash cloud.

Residents have learned to adapt to eruptions, and most volcanoes are away from residential areas. In the case of the 2014-2015 Holuhraun eruption, the region near Vatnajökull was evacuated of locals, and tourists and animals were moved from the area. There were no deaths or major injuries. The main threat was from toxins in the air, and those close to the region were asked to stay indoors and turn up their heating if they were sensitive to air quality.

Air

When there isn't an eruption, Iceland's air is some of the cleanest and purest you will experience, as pollution is low and the Gulf Stream produces a strong, steady wind that blows toxins away. The main source of pollution on the island is from industry, mainly aluminum smelters.

Water

Like the air, Iceland's water is perfectly pure. There's clean, tasty drinking water on tap and geothermally heated water that fills swimming pools and provides hot water in homes. Snow can fall in any month of the year, but large snowfalls are uncommon in the Reykjavík area, at least during the last couple of decades. Ice covers about 11 percent of the country, mostly in the form of Iceland's largest glaciers: Vatnajökull, Hofsjökull, Langjökull, and Mýrdalsjökull. Melting ice from the glaciers and snowmelt form the rivers.

Iceland's water is at the center of some of the country's tourist attractions. The man-made Blue Lagoon near Grindavík allows visitors to bathe in geothermally heated water, which soothes and heals the skin. Locals and tourists enjoy hot springs throughout the country, and spectacular waterfalls with roaring water tumble over basalt rock and earth. The largest and most visited waterfalls in Iceland are Gullfoss, Dettifoss, Goðafoss, and Skógafoss.

Northern Lights

The biggest winter attraction in Iceland is the aurora borealis (northern lights). People travel from around the world to catch a glimpse of the green, white, blue, and red lights dancing in the night sky. There's something very special about bundling up in your warmest winter gear, trekking outside main towns to avoid bright lights, and hunting for the aurora borealis. The phenomenon is caused by solar winds, which push electronic particles to collide with molecules of atmospheric gases, causing an emission of bright light. The best time to see northern lights is from September to March, and there are forecasts predicting visibility on the **national weather website** (www.vedur.is). When the forecast is favorable, it's best to drive (or take a tour bus) to a dark area and look up. Northern lights tours are offered by **Reykjavík Excursions** (www.re.is).

History

SETTLEMENT

Iceland has the distinction of being the last country in Europe to be settled. The country is known for impeccable record-keeping, and for that reason, it's known that the first permanent resident in Iceland was Ingólfur Arnarson, who built a farm in Reykjavík in the year 874. The earliest settlers were emigrants from Norway who opposed the king, Harald, due to a blood feud, and they wanted to make a new life in a new land. The Norwegians brought along their slaves from Ireland and Scotland, which means Icelanders are a blend of Norse and Celtic stock.

As word got out about the new land, within a few decades most of the coastline was claimed, with farms and fishing stations popping up. A government wasn't formed until 930, when the Alþing (parliament) was created, but in the meantime the new settlers determined that each farmstead should have a self-appointed chief. Once the Alþing was established in Þingvellir, a legislative body was elected.

CONVERSION TO CHRISTIANITY

Christianity came to Iceland, some say, by force. By the 10th century, the island faced mounting political pressure from the king of Norway to convert to Christianity or face the consequences, meaning war. As the end of the first millennium grew near, many prominent Icelanders had accepted the new faith.

By the year 1000, the Alþing was divided into two religious groups: modern Christians and pagans. The two groups were steadfast in their beliefs, and a civil war seemed likely. The law speaker, Þorgeir Þorkelsson, was called upon for a decision. (The law speaker was appointed to office and was required to recite the law during parliamentary meetings.) Þorgeir decided that Iceland would be a Christian country, but that pagans could still celebrate their rituals in the privacy of their farms. Þorgeir was baptized in Þingvellir, and Christianity became the law of the land. Christian churches were built, a bishop was established in 1056, and the majority of today's Icelanders are Christian.

DANISH RULE

Iceland remained under Norwegian kingship rule until 1380, when the death of Olav IV put an end to the Norwegian male royal line. Norway (and by extension, Iceland) became part of the Kalmar Union, along with Denmark and Sweden, with Denmark as the dominant nation. At this time, Iceland effectively became a colony of Denmark, with the king owning the land and the church's money. Iceland's government now answered to Denmark and did so for the next several hundred years.

Iceland was still very much centered on fishing and farming, and it was quite isolated from the dealings in mainland Europe. In 1602, the Danish government, which was pursuing mercantilist policies, ordered that Iceland was forbidden to trade with countries other than Denmark. The Danish trade monopoly would remain in effect until 1786.

INDEPENDENCE

Iceland began inching toward independence when it was granted a Minister of Icelandic Affairs in 1904, who would be based in Reykjavík. Hannes Hafstein was the first to serve in the minister position, and his place in Iceland's history is prominent. During this time, Iceland became more autonomous, building up Reykjavík's harbor, founding the University of Iceland, and eventually creating its own flag in 1915.

Over the next couple of decades, Iceland was taking more control of its affairs, and when World War II started, there was an economic opportunity for the island. Iceland was invited to join the Allied war effort by Great Britain, but Iceland's government refused, declaring its neutrality. Britain pushed for Iceland's cooperation, but ultimately British naval forces arrived in Iceland, began building a base near Keflavík, and occupied the country for its proximity to North America. In all, 25,000 British soldiers occupied Iceland, which created a significant number of jobs for Icelanders. The British left in 1941, but more than 40,000 American troops replaced them, continuing the economic win for Iceland. There were jobs, opportunity, an American radio station, and lots of money flowing into the tiny island nation.

Denmark took a step back from Iceland's affairs during World War II, and Icelanders eventually held a referendum on its independence. Almost 99 percent of the population voted in the referendum, 97 percent of which voted for independence. On June 17, 1944, Iceland became totally independent of Denmark. American troops maintained the Keflavík NATO base until 2006.

MODERN-DAY ICELAND

An independent Iceland plodded along, building up its fishing resources, investing in infrastructure, and looking toward the future. During years of rule by the center-right Independence Party, banks were deregulated in the early 2000s and Iceland's financial sector began taking off at a rapid pace. Iceland was being lauded for its financial acumen, but it all imploded in 2008, when the country's three major banks failed, sending Iceland into one of the deepest financial crises seen in modern Europe. Iceland is still rebuilding and recovering today.

One of the most divisive issues in Iceland has been whether to join the European Union (EU). Polls indicate that the majority of Icelanders are against joining, and the Independence/Progressive coalition that was elected in 2013 halted EU talks altogether. The debate continues as Icelanders demand a referendum on the matter, which was promised by the parties in power.

Iceland today is reaping the benefits of increased tourism. People from around the world have become aware of and infatuated with Iceland for its raw nature, volcanic eruptions, and culture.

Government and Economy

GOVERNMENT

Iceland's government dates back to the year 930, when the Alþing (parliament) was formed, but its constitution was signed on June 17, 1944, when Iceland achieved independence from Denmark. The Alþing, which consists of 63 seats, meets four days a week near Austurvöllur in the center of Reykjavík. Nine judges make up the High Court of Iceland and are appointed by the president. Iceland's president serves more of a ceremonial role, while the prime minister holds most of the executive powers. Other high-level cabinet positions are the Minister of Finance and Minister of Foreign Affairs.

Political Parties

Iceland's political parties number in double digits, with 12 parties running for seats in the 2016 election. However, in the Alþing, seven parties hold seats: Independence Party, Progressive Party, Social Democratic Alliance, Left-Green Movement, Bright Future, Pirate Party, and the Reform Party.

The Independence Party (Sjálfstæðisflokkurinn) is a center-right party that was formed in 1929 after a merger of the Conservative and Liberal parties. The current prime minister, Bjarni Benediktsson, a former lawyer, has served as leader of the party since 2009. The Independence Party was in power in the years leading up to the economic collapse of 2008. It was voted out of the majority in 2009 but regained seats, and power, in 2013.

The Social Democratic Alliance, Bright Future, Left-Green Movement, and Pirate Party are the more liberal political parties on the island. Iceland's sitting president, Guðni Th. Jóhannesson, who took office in 2016, is a historian and former docent at the University of Iceland. Guðni is unaffiliated with any political party. He replaced Ólafur Ragnar Grímsson, who served five terms.

Defense

Iceland does not have a military, but it hosted British and American troops in Keflavík during and after World War II. American troops remained in Iceland, on the NATO base, until 2006, at the height of the U.S. military involvement in Iraq and Afghanistan. Iceland's Coast Guard oversees crisis management and protection along the coasts of Iceland and has been known to participate in daring rescues at sea. The Icelandic police force consists of fewer than 1,000 officers, who maintain the peace. The crime rate is exceptionally low in Iceland, and police officers do not carry handguns.

ECONOMY

Iceland's economy is best known to tourists for taking a dive during the 2008 financial crisis. The island has rebounded from the collapse, with tourism playing a significant role in this recovery, along with alternative energy.

Banking Crisis

In early 2008, Iceland's currency began floundering compared to the euro, and that was the first international signal that there was deep trouble lurking in Iceland's financial sector. By the autumn, all three of Iceland's major banks had failed, lifting the veil on Iceland's house of cards. Following the collapse, unemployment soared, pension funds shrank, and inflation skyrocketed to more than 70 percent. Loans taken out in foreign currency became unmanageable to thousands of Icelanders, credit lines were cut off, and capital controls were put in place that restricted how much money Icelanders could move out of the country. It was dire. The IMF made an emergency loan of $2.1 billion in November 2008.

Tourism

An increase in tourism helped Iceland recover from its 2008 economic collapse. In fact, tourism is now the country's second-biggest revenue source after fish. Tourism comprises 10 percent of Iceland's GDP, and it's estimated that more than two million tourists will visit Iceland in 2017. Most of Iceland's tourists come from the United States, Great Britain, the Nordic countries, Germany, France, and Switzerland. Tourism from Asian countries is also increasing. The issue going forward is how to keep tourism sustainable and protect Iceland's land from too much traffic.

Fishing

It's no secret that fish are the lifeblood of Iceland. They nourish its residents and are Iceland's number one export. Iceland's biggest trading partners are within the European Union, which is interesting because the reason to oppose joining the EU, for many, is for Iceland to maintain complete control of its fishing stock. Cod is the most common fish export.

Energy

One of the perks of living on a volcanic island is having a hotbed of geothermal energy. About 98 percent of the island's energy comes from geothermal and hydroelectric sources, which means low costs and low pollution. The pollution that does inhabit Iceland's airspace stems from an increasing number of aluminum smelters that have popped up in the last couple of decades. Foreign aluminum providers look to Iceland for its cheap energy and vast open land. The smelters do create jobs and revenue for the country, but it's a trade-off that many Icelanders remain unhappy about. As of this writing, Iceland was in talks with the United Kingdom on how to export geothermal energy there.

Currency

Iceland maintains its own currency, as it is not a member of the European Union. The Icelandic króna has a small circulation and is pegged to the euro. Following the financial crisis, inflation soared more than 70 percent, and Iceland's currency took a hit. The uncertainty was a maddening time for many Icelanders. Inflation is still high, and exchange rates rise and fall. Capital controls were created in 2008 that limit how much money Icelanders can move out of the country, but they started being lifted in 2017.

People and Culture

POPULATION

Nearly 340,000 people call Iceland home, and more than two-thirds live in the capital city, Reykjavík, and its suburbs. Outside of Reykjavík, Hafnarfjörður, and Kopavogur, the most populated towns in Iceland include Keflavík and Selfoss in the south, Akureyri in the north, Akranes and Borgarnes in the west, and Höfn and Egilsstaðir in the east. About 90 percent of the island population is composed of native Icelanders, but the foreign-born population continues to grow with the inflow of migrant workers and refugees. Iceland is as multicultural today as it has ever been.

Native Icelanders have a genetic makeup that combines Gaelic and Norse heritage, and many Icelanders consider themselves Nordic instead of Scandinavian. Social lives center on family, as Icelanders tend to be a close-knit bunch. People often either know one another or have friends in common.

LANGUAGE

The official language of Iceland is Icelandic, which is considered a Germanic language. Icelanders like to think of their language as poetic and musical, and maintaining their tongue is an important part of Icelandic culture. Most Icelanders speak English and are happy to converse with tourists in English, but they are proud of their mother tongue and enjoy when foreign tourists give the language a go, even just a few words. The closest language to Icelandic is Faroese, which roughly 50,000 people speak, and the other close language spoken by a larger group is Norwegian. Many Icelanders can understand Norwegian, Swedish, and Danish due to some similarities. Learning Icelandic is a challenge for many foreigners because of the complex grammar and accent.

Alphabet

The Icelandic alphabet has 32 letters, including letters not known in the English language, such as Ð and Þ. The letter Ð represents the sound "th" as in "this," while Þ represents "th" as in "thin."

ICELANDIC NAMES

Iceland has a strident naming committee that must approve names parents wish to give their newborns, in the spirit of maintaining Icelandic culture. For that reason, you will find a lot of common first names, including Bjorn, Jón, Ólafur, Guðmundur, and Magnús for males, and Guðrun, Sara, and Anna for females. Very few Icelanders have surnames; instead, Iceland follows a patronymic system in which children are given their father's first name followed by -son or -dottir. If a man named Einar has a son named Johannes and a daughter named Anna, their names will be Johannes Einarsson and Anna Einarsdottir.

RELIGION

Icelanders have an interesting relationship with religion. Most of the country identifies as Lutheran (about 70 percent), but most Icelanders aren't known to attend church regularly or be very vocal about their religious beliefs. While the majority of the country identifies as Christian, Iceland is considered a progressive nation. There is no separation of church and state in Iceland; the National Church of Iceland is subsidized by Icelanders through a church tax. However, non-Lutherans can choose to have their church tax donated to designated charities.

Of Iceland's religious minorities, Catholics are the largest group at about 4 percent, and there are about 1,000 Muslims estimated to call Iceland home, as well as about 100 Jews. There is not a single synagogue in Iceland, as the Jewish population has not requested one, but a mosque was approved by Reykjavík in 2014, and construction is ongoing as of 2017. The pagan Norse religion Ásatrúarfélagið has grown in membership in recent years to nearly 4,000.

Best Festivals in Iceland

There's always something going on in Iceland—and whether it's the Viking Festival in June celebrating the country's roots, or the huge Iceland Airwaves music festival in the autumn, there's something for everyone.

February
Sónar Reykjavík (Reykjavík): This three-day music festival in mid-February features local and international rock, pop, and electronic bands.
Reykjavík Food & Fun Festival (Reykjavík): During this three-day festival at the end of February, world-renowned chefs occupy kitchens at trendy Reykjavík restaurants, using fresh local ingredients and lots of imagination.

March
DesignMarch (HönnunarMars) (Reykjavík): Typically held in early March over four days, DesignMarch showcases the newest and best Icelandic design in pop-up shops, lectures, and fun events around the city.

April
Reykjavík Blues Festival (Blúshátíð í Reykjavík) (Reykjavík): For a week in early April, blues music enthusiasts from around the world descend on Reykjavík for this annual festival that features international musicians and local artists.
AK-Extreme (Akureyri): Dedicated to winter extreme sports, AK-Extreme is an annual snowboard and music festival held in the northern city of Akureyri over four days in mid-April.

May
Reykjavík Arts Festival (Listahátíð í Reykjavík) (Reykjavík): For two weeks over late May and early June, Reykjavík is treated to exhibitions and outdoor installations of local and international artists.

FOLKLORE

Icelanders have a spiritual connection to nature, which has been depicted through literature, paintings, and stories about the *huldufólk* or "hidden people." It's easy to understand why stories of *huldufólk* are prevalent once you experience the otherworldly nature of Iceland, including northern lights, crazy rock formations, howling wind, and desolate lava fields where it feels that anything can happen. Many of the hidden people stories originate in the lava fields, where unexplained phenomena, like broken farm equipment, could be explained away by saying "it must be the *huldufólk*." Indeed, Iceland's hidden people live among the rocks, and certain rocks are deemed "*huldufólk* churches." It's easy to dismiss the idea of hidden people, especially when the term is loosely translated as elves, but many Icelanders are not willing to deny the existence of *huldufólk*. Does that mean that all Icelanders believe that elves physically walk among their human neighbors? Of course not. But it is part of their history and culture, and many Icelanders have a sense of humor about the foreign notion of *huldufólk*.

June

Viking Festival (Hafnarfjörður): Just outside Reykjavík, the annual Viking Festival in mid-June has fun reenactments of fights with traditional dress and weaponry, as well as food, music, and a market. The weeklong festival is great for kids.

August

Reykjavík Jazz Festival (Jazzhátíð Reykjavíkur) (Reykjavík): It may seem unexpected, but Icelanders have an affinity for jazz music, and they put on a great annual festival over five days in mid-August that features local and international musicians.

Culture Night (Menningarnótt) (Reykjavík): Held at the end of August, this daylong event is the biggest and most popular festival in Iceland, with more than 100,000 people participating. There's live music, food, and art to celebrate the end of the summer and Iceland's rich culture.

September

Reykjavík International Film Festival (Reykjavík): Beginning at the end of September, this 11-day festival showcases short films, documentaries, and features from more than 40 countries.

November

Iceland Airwaves (Reykjavík): The largest music festival of the year hits Iceland in late October and early November. More than 200 local and international artists perform at the five-day festival, which has attracted bands including Kraftwerk, Flaming Lips, and local band Of Monsters and Men.

ARTS

Music

Music plays an important role in Icelandic society. There's still an emphasis on children learning to play instruments, and there are music schools around the country. It seems that everyone in Iceland is in at least one band. The earliest Icelandic music is called *rímur,* which is a sort of chanting style of singing that could include lyrics ranging from religious themes to descriptions of nature. Choirs are also very common in Iceland, and there are frequent performances in schools and churches that are usually well attended by the community.

As for modern music, Iceland boasts quite a few acts that have gained a following abroad. Of course, there's Björk, who put Iceland on the musical map back in the 1980s with her band, the Sugarcubes, and later her solo career. Icelanders tend to be quite proud of Björk, as both an artist and an environmentalist. Sigur Rós became an indie favorite, and the band has been recording since 1994. Of Monsters and Men, Kaleo, Ólafur Arnalds,

Amiina, Samaris, and GusGus are taking the world by storm. Reykjavík has cool venues in which to check out local bands and DJs, and some great record shops to pick up the newest and latest Icelandic releases.

Literature

Iceland has a rich literary history. The sagas, considered the best-known examples of Icelandic literature, are stories in prose describing events that took place in Iceland in the 10th and 11th centuries, during the so-called Saga Age. Focused on history, especially genealogical and family history, the sagas reflect the conflicts that arose within the societies of the second and third generations of Icelandic settlers. The authors of the sagas are unknown; *Egil's Saga* is believed to have been written by Snorri Sturluson, a 13th-century descendant of the saga's hero, but this remains uncertain. Widely read in school, the sagas are celebrated as an important part of Iceland's history.

Icelanders are voracious readers and love to write novels, prose, and poetry. The nation's most celebrated author is Halldór Laxness, who won a Nobel Prize for Literature in 1951 for his cherished novel *Independent People*. His tales have been translated into several languages and center on themes near and dear to Icelanders—nature, love, travel, and adventure. Other authors who have been translated into English (and other languages) include Sjón, Arnaldur Indriðason, and Einar Már Guðmundsson, among scores of others.

Crafts (Knitting)

Icelanders have been knitting for centuries, and it remains a common hobby today. Icelandic sheep have been the source of wool that's been keeping Icelanders warm for generations, and a traditional, modern sweater design emerged in the 1950s or so in the form of the *lopapeysa*. A *lopapeysa* has a distinctive yoke design around the neck opening, and the sweater comes in a variety of colors, with the most common being brown, gray, black, and off-white. Icelanders knit with *lopi* yarn, which contains both hairs and fleece of Icelandic sheep. The yarn is not spun, making it more difficult to work with than spun yarn, but the texture and insulation are unmistakable.

Essentials

Transportation

GETTING THERE
Air

Keflavík International Airport (KEF, tel. 354/425-6000, www.kefairport. is), about 50 minutes west of Reykjavík, frequently gets kudos for being one of the best airports in Europe, and the plaudits are well deserved. Flying into Iceland is a pretty seamless experience. The country's main carrier, **Icelandair** (www.icelandair.com), serves more than 30 destinations in the United States, Canada, and Europe. Iceland's accessibility has been the country's main selling point as a travel destination because it is just five hours from New York City and about three hours from London. Icelandair cleverly introduced an option years ago that allows North American travelers going on to Europe to stop over in Iceland for no extra cost. You can spend a couple of days or more exploring Iceland, and then continue on to your destination in Europe. The summer season is obviously the most expensive, with round-trip tickets that could exceed $1,000 from North America. Icelandair offers great deals during the winter months, when you can grab a round-trip ticket for around $500. **WOW Air** (www.wowair. com) expanded to the U.S. market in 2016, offering low-cost flights to Iceland. In addition to Europe and Canada, the airline flies from Boston, Chicago, Cincinnati, Cleveland, Detroit, Los Angeles, Miami, New York, San Francisco, St. Louis, and Washington DC. One-way fares can be as cheap as $99.

Sea

For those traveling from mainland Europe, a ferry can be a great option, especially if you want to bring a car, camper, or bicycle for the trip. **Smyril Line** (www.smyril-line.fo) is a Faroese company that runs the ferry *Norröna,* which goes to Iceland from Denmark, Norway, and the Faroe Islands. The ferry drops you off in Seyðisfjörður, in East Iceland, which is convenient for those traveling with cars and who want to spend time in the countryside. But, if you want to stay in the south, where Reykjavík and Golden Circle attractions are, a ferry may not be the best option. The timetable tends to change frequently, so check the website for the latest information.

Previous: a herd of sheep crossing the road in Iceland; traditional Icelandic sweaters for sale.

VISAS AND PASSPORTS

Visitors to Iceland must have a valid passport that will not expire within three months of your scheduled departure. Tourists from the United States, Canada, Australia, and New Zealand do not need a visa if they are traveling to Iceland for fewer than 90 days. If you want to stay longer, you need to apply for a residence permit at the Icelandic immigration office (www. utl.is). For Europeans, Iceland is part of the Schengen Agreement, which allows free travel between Iceland and European Economic Area (EEA) and European Union (EU) countries; visas are not necessary.

EMBASSIES
Icelandic Embassies

Iceland has embassies in a number of countries, including:

- **Canada:** 360 Albert St., Suite 710, Ottawa, ON K1R 7X7, tel. 613/482-1944, www.iceland.is/ca
- **United Kingdom:** 2A Hans St, London SW1X 0JE, tel. 20/7259-3999, www.iceland.is/uk
- **United States:** 2900 K St. NW, Suite 509, Washington, DC 20007, tel. 202/265-6653, www.iceland.is/us

Foreign Embassies in Iceland

If you have an emergency while traveling in Iceland and require assistance (for example, if you lose your passport), contact your embassy for help. Embassies in Reykjavík include:

- **Canada:** Túngata 14, tel. 354/575-6500, rkjvk@international.gc.ca
- **United Kingdom:** Laufásvegur 31, tel. 354/550-5100, info@britishembassy.is
- **United States:** Laufásvegur 21, tel. 354/595-2200, reykjavikconsular@state.gov

CUSTOMS

Getting through customs in Iceland is quite easy compared to most other countries in Europe.

Travelers can import duty-free alcoholic beverages and tobacco products as follows: 1 liter of spirits, 1 liter of wine, and 1 carton or 250g of tobacco products; or 1 liter of spirits, 6 liters of beer, and 1 carton or 250g of tobacco products; or 1.5 liters of wine, 6 liters of beer, and 1 carton or 250g of tobacco products; or 3 liters wine and 1 carton or 250g of tobacco products. The minimum age for bringing alcoholic beverages into Iceland is 20 years; for tobacco, it's 18 years.

Iceland has a zero-tolerance policy on drugs, and all meat, raw-egg products, and unpasteurized dairy will be confiscated.

For additional information, visit the official customs website (www. tollur.is).

TYPICAL FARE

The description of Icelandic food that you get depends on whom you ask, although it can't be disputed that fish and lamb take center stage. Typical fare can range from light to hearty. Local produce means what can survive outdoors (potatoes, rhubarb, moss) and what is grown in greenhouses (tomatoes, cucumbers, broccoli, etc.). Most of Iceland's food is imported, and it isn't cheap.

Local fish includes cod (fresh/salted), salmon, lobster, mussels, halibut, trout, and haddock. A classic Icelandic dish is whitefish cooked in a white sauce with potatoes and onions. A popular snack is hardfish, which is like a whitefish jerky, where the fish is dried and seasoned.

As for meat, lamb is the most prevalent, but there is plenty of beef, pork, and chicken in the Icelandic diet. Some Icelanders also indulge in horse and whale meat as well.

Hot dogs are wildly popular among Icelanders. Called *pylsur,* Icelandic hot dogs are done up in a traditional bun with chopped onions, mustard, ketchup, crispy fried onions, and pickled mayonnaise. They're delicious.

Dairy is an important part of Icelanders' diets, including milk, cheese, butter, and the yogurt-like soft cheese called *skyr,* which you should try. It's very tasty and chock-full of protein. Icelanders are also known to eat ice cream all year long, despite the weather. There are quite a few popular ice cream shops around Reykjavík, and the ice cream sections in supermarkets offer an astounding number of locally produced choices.

Once a year, Icelanders celebrate the traditional foods of the nation, which sustained their ancestors through the ages. The winter festival, called Þorrablót, features *svið* (singed lamb head), blood pudding, lamb intestines and stomach, ram's testicles, fermented shark, seal flippers, hardfish, and rye bread. The food that gets the most attention from foreigners is rotten shark or *hákarl,* which is meat from Greenland shark. The flesh is put through an interesting process, where it is buried for at least two months and then is hung for another three or four months to cure. If you dare, *hákarl* is available in small containers for sale. It is an experience you will not forget—if not the taste, then definitely the smell.

FINDING A RESTAURANT

Reykjavík is home to some excellent fine-dining establishments and casual eateries, but eating cheaply in Reykjavík, or on the island as a whole, is not easy. Hours tend to change depending on the season, but for the most part restaurants open their doors for lunch around 11:30am, and kitchens tend to close around 10pm.

Outside of Reykjavík and Akureyri, you will find a lot of fish and lamb restaurants that focus on local cuisine, but inside the two main cities, you have a lot to choose from. You will find sushi, tapas, Indian, hamburger

International cuisine has been growing in popularity over the last 20 years, and new and interesting spots are always cropping up.

DRINKING

The water in Iceland is pure and some of the tastiest in the world. Drinking from the tap is common and safe, and bottled water is frowned upon. Iceland is also a coffee-drinking nation. If you're a tea drinker, you will find some basic choices in coffee shops, but Icelanders are crazy about their coffee.

As for alcohol, Icelanders do have a reputation for indulging, but given the expensive prices, beer is the drink of choice when going out to a bar. And, believe it or not, beer is still relatively new to Iceland. A countrywide alcohol ban went into effect in 1915; the ban was relaxed in phases, with first wine and then strong liquors permitted, and beer eventually became legal to sell in 1989. Outside of bars, alcohol is available only at the government-run shops called Vínbúðin.

Accommodations

HOTELS

Iceland is not known for posh hotels offering every luxury that you desire. However, there is a good mix of "upscale" accommodations, mid-level boutiques, and budget hotels. The "fanciest" options on the island are in Reykjavík, namely 101 Hotel and Hótel Borg, which cater to guests who are willing to pay for top-notch service and amenities. Reykjavík also has midrange boutique or family-run options if you are looking for something a bit more formal than a guesthouse.

Outside of Reykjavík, hotels tend to be of the local chain-hotel ilk in the form of **Fosshotels** (www.fosshotel.is), **Hótel Edda** (www.hoteledda. is), and **Icelandair Hótels** (www.icelandairhotels.is). They are clean, comfortable, and reliable options.

When they compare hotel prices to those in other European countries, some tourists feel that they don't get their money's worth. In fairness, Iceland is a more popular destination than it was 20 years ago, but it's still not meant to be a budget destination. In short, accommodations do cost a lot. Be prepared for slightly shocking rates, especially in the summer months.

GUESTHOUSES

The most prevalent form of accommodations on the island is the guesthouse setup. Guesthouses range from comfortable bed-and-breakfasts that offer shared bathrooms and cooking facilities to more design-conscious options that are chic, modern, and fun. Some guesthouses in Reykjavík can still have "hotel-like" prices, as the competition for scoring a room in the high season has become almost a contact sport. Outside Reykjavík, however, guesthouses could be a good way to save a little money, depending on where you book. Always book a room in advance, as it's not recommended to leave where you will lay your head to chance.

HOSTELS

Hostels are another great option for the budget traveler, but as in guesthouses, beds tend to fill up, so make sure you book far in advance, especially in the summer. Some hostels in Reykjavík, like Kex Hostel and Loft Hostel, cater to young, music-conscious travelers, and beds are almost an afterthought. There is frequently live music in the lounge areas, and the bar is always packed with locals and tourists. Other hostel options cater to a more mature crowd looking to avoid the high hotel rates. Hlemmur Square would be a good option for those travelers. Outside of Reykjavík, hostels are prevalent and it's key to book ahead.

SLEEPING BAG ACCOMMODATIONS

Some guesthouses and hostels around Iceland offer travelers sleeping bag accommodations, which can be great for the budget traveler. For a low price, guests are allowed to sleep in their sleeping bags and have access to shared bathroom facilities.

Travel Tips

WHAT TO PACK

How you pack depends on where you plan to go and what you're going to do on the island. If you're going for a "city-break" long weekend to Reykjavík, you can afford to pack light; however, if you plan on an extended stay that includes camping, packing light is not an option. Here are some suggestions and tips for your time in Iceland.

Clothing

The key to dressing warm and being comfortable in Iceland is layers. Depending on the weather, it can be cotton T-shirt, fleece or sweater, parka or windbreaker, and perhaps a hat, scarf, and gloves. If it's summer and the sun is shining, it's common to see locals wearing a T-shirt in 15°C (60°F) weather. It's important to keep comfortable and add layers if the temperature warrants it. If you're out hiking, wearing waterproof gear along with proper hiking attire is key. Make sure fabrics are breathable and comfortable and underlayers are cotton. Formal attire in Iceland is reserved for work or funerals, but if you want to bring a nice outfit along for a "fancy" dinner, by all means, pack something, but you won't find stringent dress codes anywhere on this island. Lastly, a bathing suit is necessary. Even if you think you won't take a dip in a pool or hot spring, the temptation might be too great. Pack at least one.

Outerwear
Because the temperature varies so much depending on time of day, season, and where you are in the country, it's a good idea to bring a hat, scarf, and gloves. As for jackets, the best advice is to bring something waterproof; whether it's a windbreaker for summer or a parka for winter, you are likely to encounter rain at some point on your trip. If you need to go shopping for warmer layers in Iceland, expect to pay. Clothes are not cheap in Iceland.

Footwear
Again, if you are staying in Reykjavík for the duration of your trip, and don't plan to climb mountains, you don't need to invest in an expensive pair of hiking boots. That said, if you do plan to be outdoors quite a bit, hiking boots are a great idea. You will need a pair of shoes that can withstand rain, rocks, ice, mud, puddles, sand, and sometimes snow. It's recommended to buy boots in your home country because shoes can be expensive in Iceland, and it's not the best idea to break in a brand-new pair of boots if you plan to do a lot of walking and/or climbing. Comfort is key. Socks are also important to consider. You want socks that are breathable yet thick enough to keep you comfortable in your shoes/boots.

TIME ZONE
Iceland uses Greenwich mean time (GMT). However, the country does not observe daylight saving time, so Iceland is either four or five hours ahead of New York time, depending on the time of year.

As for the amount of daylight, what you've heard is true. The summers are full of long days, and darkness reigns supreme in the winter. To give you an idea of what that means, here are daylight hours for Reykjavík at different times of year:

- January 1: sunrise 11:20am, sunset 3:45pm
- April 1: sunrise 6:45am, sunset 8:20pm
- July 1: sunrise 3:05am, sunset midnight
- October 1: sunrise 7:30am, sunset 7pm

WEIGHTS AND MEASURES
Iceland uses the metric system. With regard to electricity, the standard voltage is 230 V and the standard frequency is 50 Hz. The power sockets that are used are type F, for plugs with two round pins. If you forget to bring an adapter, they can be purchased in most bookstores and tourist shops.

ACCESS FOR TRAVELERS WITH DISABILITIES

Iceland has taken great strides in making as many tourist-related sites as wheelchair friendly as possible. Visitors in wheelchairs will find that most museums, swimming pools, and restaurants provide access, as do transportation services. For instance, Keflavík International Airport and all domestic airlines can accommodate travelers in wheelchairs, and many buses come with automatic ramps to allow for easy boarding.

For more information on accessible travel, get in touch with the organization Þekkingarmiðstöð Sjálfsbjargar (tel. 354/550-0118, www.thekkingarmidstod.is). While the website is almost entirely in Icelandic only, information on traveling in Iceland has been translated into English (www.thekkingarmidstod.is/adgengi/accessible-tourism-in-iceland), and employees are happy to assist in English.

For information on services available to deaf travelers, contact the Icelandic Association of the Deaf (www.deaf.is), and for services for the sight-impaired, contact the Icelandic Association of the Blind (www.blind.is).

TRAVELING WITH CHILDREN

Children are the center of Icelandic society, and tourists traveling with children will feel right at home, whether in restaurants or museums or on child-appropriate tours. The island is a safe place for children, and many foreign travelers raise an eyebrow at how carefree parents can appear—whether it's a child walking around a shop, or an unaccompanied pram outside a coffeehouse. It's not irresponsible parenting, just a reflection on how safe a society Iceland is. While Iceland is safe, it needs to be said to always take care to watch out for the elements, whether it's high winds, a slippery surface, or cracks in a walking path.

As for attractions and restaurants, there are frequently child rates for museums and tours, and children's options on menus. Discounts can be as great as 50 percent for children under the age of 16.

WOMEN TRAVELING ALONE

Iceland is regularly ranked as being one of the best countries in the world in which to be a woman and a mother. Icelanders are proud to have elected the first woman president in the world as well as the first openly gay prime minister (a woman). However, Iceland is not a utopia. Women are subject to incidents of theft, intimidation, and physical violence. Always keep your wits about you, and if you are a victim of crime, contact the police at the emergency number 112.

GAY AND LESBIAN TRAVELERS

Iceland is a leader in equality, and Reykjavík is one of the most gay-friendly cities in Europe. What many travelers find refreshing is that there is not just tolerance for gay, lesbian, bisexual, and transgendered individuals, but overwhelming love and acceptance of their fellow Icelanders. For instance, the gay pride festival, **Reykjavík Pride,** which takes place every August, attracts approximately 100,000 participants, for a country of just 320,000 people. Think about that. As for laws, the LGBT community is protected from discrimination, gay marriage was legalized in 2010, and hate crimes are few and far between. For such a small population, it's hard to say there's a "gay scene," but there is one gay bar in Reykjavík, Kiki Queer Bar. More information can be found at the **Pink Iceland** website (www. pinkiceland.is).

Information and Services

TOURIST INFORMATION

Visit Iceland (www.visiticeland.com) is the main tourist information website for the country. The website has information on accommodations and activities for each region in Iceland.

MAPS

To properly navigate Iceland, you need maps. That's a given. Lucky for you, they are available all over the island. You can pick up all-inclusive maps for the entire island as well as regional maps, road maps, and hiking maps at tourist information centers, bookstores, and gas stations. If you have the chance to purchase maps before your trip, do so, as they will likely be a lot cheaper in your home country. However, if you plan to stay in Reykjavík for the duration of your trip, it's not necessary to buy a map because quite a few free maps do a nice job detailing downtown Reykjavík.

HEALTH AND SAFETY

Medical Services

The Icelandic health-care system is top-notch, with hospitals in each large town and health clinics in smaller villages and hamlets. Most doctors, nurses, and emergency medical staff speak English. Non-EU citizens must pay for health services provided. If you are having a medical emergency, dial the number 112. Pharmacies (called *apótek*) hold everything from prescription medication to aspirin. Some tourists from North America find it frustrating that cold medicine and aspirin cannot be bought in supermarkets, just at the pharmacy. Pharmacies are typically open 10am-9pm Monday-Friday, 10am-4pm Saturday, and are closed on Sunday and public holidays.

Weather

Weather is the number one safety concern in Iceland, trumping everything from violent crime to volcanic eruptions. The main danger is how fast weather can change. It could be a bright, sunny day when you head out on a trek in the highlands, but there could be a storm brewing that will bring high winds, rain, hail, and snow. And the storm could pass as quickly as it arrived. The joke among locals is that if you don't like the weather in Iceland, wait five minutes. The best defense against inclement weather is to closely monitor weather forecasts and obey advisories. You can check frequently updated forecasts at www.vedur.is. Icelanders deal with the weather by being flexible and never confirming plans far in advance. They learn to adapt after a lifetime of battling gale-force winds.

Temperatures in Iceland can vary, but on average Reykjavík's winter season is warmer than New York City's. That said, always dress for the environment and the activity you are about to embark on. If you are staying within Reykjavík's city limits, dress comfortably with layers and waterproof gear. If you're out in the countryside in the evening, have a hat, scarf, gloves, and warm gear at the ready. It can get chilly and hypothermia can set in quickly.

Crime

Crime is quite low in Iceland and is mostly limited to theft and vandalism; violent crime is rare. Be vigilant in protecting your possessions (especially bicycles) and trust your instincts. If you're out at night on Laugavegur in downtown Reykjavík on weekends, you might encounter loud and drunk locals or tourists. Don't engage with drunken people; continue about your business. If you are a victim of a crime, contact the police by dialing the emergency number, 112; all police officers are proficient in English.

MONEY

Iceland is not a cheap place to visit. Don't be fooled by the news stories that declared Iceland cut prices to accommodate tourists after its economic crisis of 2008. That period was brief, and Iceland remains an expensive destination. Prices on accommodations, food, gas, and everyday necessities remain high. Here is a list showing prices of common items.

- Milk (1 L): 149ISK
- Loaf of bread: 344ISK
- Dozen eggs: 623ISK
- Apples (1 kg): 323ISK
- Potatoes (1 kg): 278ISK
- Coke/Pepsi: 288ISK
- Meal for two: 12,000ISK
- Domestic beer: 1,100ISK
- Bottle of wine: 2,400ISK
- Pack of cigarettes: 1,300ISK
- Bus ticket (one-way): 440ISK
- Gasoline (1 L): 198ISK

Currency

The official currency of Iceland is the króna (abbreviated kr or ISK). The króna fluctuates often; at the time of writing, the exchange rate was 105ISK to US$1.

There are banknotes in the amount of 500, 1,000, 5,000, and 10,000 and coins in the amount of 1, 5, 10, 50, and 100 kronur. Coins are handy for having exact change for the bus.

Currency exchange is available at the airport and banks as well as tourist information offices. ATMs are available at all banks as well as supermarkets and other shops.

Banks

Banking hours are 9:15am-4pm Monday-Friday, and ATMs are available 24/7. There may be a limit on the amount of cash you can withdraw per your home bank's policy.

Credit Cards

Your best bet to get the most favorable exchange is to use your credit card. Cash overall is not a popular payment method; locals are known to use debit and credit cards for just about every transaction. Using plastic is so common in Iceland that many tourists will not need cash for anything; you can pay for parking, public toilets, and even campsite fees with a credit card. However, you may want to carry a little cash on you if you plan on tipping a guide for an excursion; guides will gladly accept any currency.

Tax-Free Shopping

As tourists encounter high prices for everything from accommodations to food, it only seems fair that you get a break when it comes to shopping.

A refund of local Value-Added Tax (VAT) is available to all visitors in Iceland. The refund will result in a reduction of up to 15 percent of the retail price, provided departure from Iceland is within three months after the date of purchase.

The fine print is that the refund does not apply to food or accommodations and the purchase must exceed 4,000ISK (VAT included) per store. Shops will provide you with a tax-free form (ask the store clerk for a "tax-free check"). Make sure you secure the forms and redeem the rebate at the cash-refund office at Keflavík Airport before your flight. There, you will get an immediate cash refund.

You can also submit the receipts and paperwork by mail for a rebate on your credit card. This, of course, can take considerably longer.

Tipping

Tipping is very new to Iceland. Workers in bars, restaurants, and hotels, as well as taxi drivers, earn a living wage and are not dependent on tips. In recent years, tip jars have cropped up in coffeehouses and bars, but it's just tourists who tend to tip.

COMMUNICATIONS AND MEDIA

Telephone

The country code for Iceland is 354. There are no area codes; if you are calling from within the country, just dial the seven-digit phone number and you will connect.

Icelanders love their mobile phones, and for that reason pay phones became obsolete several years ago. You can purchase international phone cards at local shops (called *sjoppas*) as well as at post offices and gas stations. SIM cards are also available from providers **Vodafone** (www.vodafone.is) and **Siminn** (www.siminn.is) and can be purchased from phone retail shops, gas stations, and the airport.

Cell phone coverage in the countryside is surprisingly strong.

Internet Access

Iceland is wired, with Wi-Fi hot spots all over the country. Hotels typically have free Wi-Fi, as do many coffeehouses.

Media

Given its small population, it's refreshing to see Iceland as such a die-hard newspaper town. Locals have several Icelandic-language print publications and websites to choose from, but publishers haven't forgotten about English-language readers. The *Reykjavík Grapevine* (www.grapevine.is) is the unofficial guide to music, museum exhibitions, restaurant reviews, and just about every cultural event in the city. The website is updated daily, and the free print edition comes out every two weeks in the summer and monthly in the winter. *Iceland Review* (www.icelandreview.com) is the main English-language glossy magazine on the island. You will find in-depth features on travel, culture, and business issues as well as gorgeous photography.

RUV (www.ruv.is) is Iceland's national public-service broadcasting organization, which consists of one television channel and two radio stations. RUV's television programs include news, dramas, and documentaries, as well as programming from foreign countries, including the United States, Denmark, and Sweden.

Resources

Glossary

austur: east
bær: farm
bíll: car
bíó: movie theater
bjarg: rock, cliff
dalur: valley
ey: island
fjall: mountain
fjörður: fjord
fljót: river
flugvöllur: airport
foss: waterfall
gata: street
geysir: erupting hot spring
gistiheimilið: guesthouse
herbergi: room
hestur: horse
höfn: harbor
hradbanki: ATM
hraun: lava field
huldufólk: hidden people
Ísland: Iceland
jökull: glacier
kirkja: church
kort: map
laug: swimming pool
lopapeysa: Icelandic knitted sweater
lundi: puffin
norður: north
safn: museum
sími: telephone
stræti: street
strætó: bus
suður: south
sumar: summer

tjörn: pond
torg: town square
vatn: water
vedur: weather
vestur: west
vetur: winter

Icelandic Phrasebook

Icelandic is not the easiest language to understand. It's a North Germanic language that is related to Norwegian, Danish, and Swedish, but it has the added difficulty of declensions that the other languages lack. Icelandic nouns are declined in four cases, which stumps many people. Fortunately, just about everyone in Iceland speaks English.

PRONUNCIATION

Pronunciation can be very tricky, but Icelanders are thrilled when tourists give their language a shot. Be warned, though; if you attempt to speak an Icelandic phrase, your accent will tell them you're a foreigner, and they most likely will answer you in English.

Vowels

Some vowels in Icelandic have accent marks that modify the sound of each vowel. Vowels can come in long or short forms. In Icelandic, all vowels can be long or short. Vowels are long when they are in single-syllable words or when they form the penultimate syllable in two-syllable words.

A a like the "a" in "land"
Á á like "ow" in "cow"
E e like the "e" in "set"
É é like "ye" in "yet"
I i like "i" in "sit"
Í í like "ee" in "feet"
O o like the "o" in "not"
Ó ó like the "o" in "flow"
U u like the "u" in "put"
Ú ú like the "oo" in "soon"
Y y like the "i" in "sit"
Ý ý like the "ee" in "feet"
Æ æ like the "i" in "file"
Ö ö like the "ur" in "lure"

Consonants

Ð ð like "th" in "this"
J j like "y" in "year"

R r rolled, like Spanish "r"
Þ þ like "th" in "that"

BASIC AND COURTEOUS EXPRESSIONS

Hello *Halló*
Good morning *Góðan dag*
Good evening *Gott kvold*
How are you? *Hvað segir þú?*
Very well, thank you *Mjog gott, takk fyrir*
Good *Allt gott*
Not OK, bad *Ekki okei*
So-so *Bara fint*
OK *Allt í lagí*
And you? *En þú?*
Thank you *Takk fyrir*
Goodbye *Bless*
Nice to see you *Gaman að sjo þig*
See you later *Sjamust*
Please *Takk*
Yes *Ja*
No *Nei*
I don't know. *Ég skil ekki.*
Just a moment. *Augnablik.*
Excuse me. *Afsakið.*
What is your name? *Hvað heiti þu?*
Do you speak English? *Talar þú ensku?*
I don't speak Icelandic well. *Ég tala ekki íslensku vel.*
I don't understand. *Ég skil ekki.*
How do you say … in Icelandic? *Hvernig segir þú … á íslensku?*
My name is … . *Ég heiti … .*
What's your name? *Hvað heitir þú?*

TERMS OF ADDRESS

I *ég*
you *þú*
he/him *hann*
she/her *hún*
we *við*
they *þeir*
girl *stelpa*
boy *strakur*
man *madur*
woman *kona*
wife *eiginkona*
husband *eiginmaður*
friend *vinur*

son *sonur*
daughter *dóttir*
brother *bróðir*
sister *systir*
father *pabbi*
mother *mamma*
grandfather *afi*
grandmother *amma*

FOOD

I'm hungry. *Ég er svangur.*
menu *matseðil*
May I have ...? *Get ég fengið ...?*
glass *glas*
fork *gaffall*
knife *hnífur*
spoon *skeið*
breakfast *morgunmatur*
lunch *hádegisverður*
dinner *kvöldmatur*
the check *reikninginn*
soda *gos*
coffee *kaffi*
tea *te*
water *vatn*
beer *bjór*
wine *vín*
white wine *hvítvín*
red wine *rauðvín*
milk *mjólk*
juice *safi*
cream *rjómi*
sugar *sykur*
eggs *eggjum*
cheese *osti*
yogurt *jógúrt*
almonds *möndlu*
cake *kaka*
bread *brauð*
butter *smjör*
salt *salt*
pepper *pipar*
garlic *hvítlaukur*
salad *salat*
vegetables *grænmeti*
carrot *gulrót*

corn *korn*
cucumber *agúrka*
lettuce *kál*
mushroom *sveppir*
onion *laukur*
potato *kartöflu*
spinach *spinat*
tomato *tómatar*
fruit *ávöxtum*
apple *epli*
orange *appelsína*
fish *fiski*
meat *kjöti*
lamb *lamb*
beef *nautakjöti*
chicken *kjúklingi*
pork *svínakjöt*
bacon *beikon*
ham *skinka*

ACCOMMODATIONS

hotel *hótel*
guesthouse *gistihúsið*
Is there a room? *Áttu laus herbergi?*
May I see the room first? *Má ég sjá herbergið fyrst?*
What is the rate? *Hvað kostar það?*
Is there something cheaper? *Ódýrara herbergi?*
single room *einsmanns herbergi*
double room *tveggjamanna herbergi*
bathroom *klósetti*
shower *sturtu*
towels *handklæði*
soap *sapa*
toilet paper *salernispappír*
sheets *rúmfötum*
key *lykill*
heater *hitari*
manager *framkvæmdastjóri*

SHOPPING

money *peningar*
What is the exchange rate? *Hvað er gengið á?*
Do you accept credit cards? *Tekur þú greiðslukort?*
How much does it cost? *Hvað kostar það?*
expensive *dýr*
cheap *ódýr*

more *meira*
less *minna*
a little *smá*
too much *of mikið*

HEALTH

Help me! *Hjálp!*
I am ill. *Ég er veikur.*
I need a doctor. *Ég þarf lækni.*
hospital *sjúkrahús*
pharmacy *apótek*
pain *verkir*
fever *hiti*
headache *höfuðverkur*
stomachache *magaverki*
burn *brunablettur*
cramp *krampa*
nausea *ógleði*
vomiting *uppköst*
antibiotic *sýklalyf*
pill *pilla*
aspirin *aspirín*
ointment *smyrsli*
cotton *bómull*
condoms *smokkur*
toothbrush *tannbursta*
toothpaste *tannkrem*
dentist *tannlæknir*

TRANSPORTATION

Where is the ...? *Hvar er ...?*
How do I get to ...? *Hvernig kemst ég til ...?*
the bus station *strætóstöðin*
the bus stop *strætóstopp*
Where is the bus going? *Hvert fer þessi strætó/rúta?*
taxi *taxi*
boat *bátur*
airport *flugvöllurinn*
I'd like a ticket to ... *Einn miða, aðra leiðina til ...*
round-trip to ... *Einn miða, báðar leiðir til ...*
Stop here. *Hætta hér.*
I want to rent a car. *Get ég leigt bíl.*
entrance *inngangur*
exit *útgangur*
to the; toward the *til*
right *hægri*

left *vinstri*
straight ahead *beint áfram*
past the ... *framhjá ...*
before the ... *á undan ...*
opposite the ... *á móti ...*
Watch for the ... *Leita að ...*
intersection *gatnamót*
street *stræti*
north; south *norður; suður*
east; west *austur; vestur*

STREET SIGNS

Stop *Stans*
One Way *Einstefna*
Yield *Biðskylda*
No Parking *Engin Bílastæði*
Speed Limit *Hámarkshraði*

AT THE GAS STATION

gas station *bensínstöð*
gasoline (petrol) *bensín*
diesel *disel*
garage *verkstæði*
air *loft*
water *vatn*
oil change *olíu breyting*
tow truck *draga vörubíl*

VERBS

to buy *að kaupa*
to eat *að borða*
to climb *að klifra*
to do or make *að gera*
to go *að fara*
to love *að elska*
to want *að vilja*
to need *að þurfa*
to read *að lesa*
to write *að skrifa*
to stop *að hætta*
to arrive *til koma*
to stay *að vera*
to leave *að fara*
to look for *að leita*
to give *að gefa*

to carry *að bera*
to have *að hafa*

NUMBERS

zero *null*
one *einn*
two *tveir*
three *prir*
four *fjorir*
five *fimm*
six *sex*
seven *sjo*
eight *atta*
nine *niu*
10 *tiu*
11 *ellefu*
12 *tólf*
13 *þrettán*
14 *fjórtán*
15 *fimmtán*
16 *sextán*
17 *sautján*
18 *átján*
19 *nítján*
20 *tuttugu*
21 *tuttugu og einn*
30 *prjatiu*
40 *fjorutiu*
50 *fimmtiu*
60 *sextiu*
70 *sjotiu*
80 *attatiu*
90 *niutiu*
100 *hundrað*
101 *hundrað og einn*
200 *tvö hundruð*
500 *fimm hundrað*
1,000 *þúsund*
100,000 *hundrað þúsund*
1,000,000 *milljón*

TIME

What time is it? *Hvað er klukkan?*
It's one o'clock. *Klukkan er eitt.*
morning *morgunn*
afternoon *eftir hádegi*

evening *kvöld*
night *nótt*
midnight *miðnætti*

DAYS AND MONTHS

Monday *mánudagur*
Tuesday *þriðjudagur*
Wednesday *miðvikudagur*
Thursday *fimmtudagur*
Friday *föstudagur*
Saturday *laugardagur*
Sunday *sunnudagur*
day *dagur*
today *í dag*
tomorrow *a morgun*
yesterday *í gær*
January *janúar*
February *febrúar*
March *mars*
April *april*
May *mai*
June *juni*
July *juli*
August *ágúst*
September *september*
October *október*
November *nóvember*
December *desember*
early *snemma*
late *seint*
later *seinna*
before *áður en*

Suggested Reading

Guðmundsson, Einar Már. *Angels of the Universe*. 1997. This is a startling tale of a young man struggling with mental illness, set in Iceland in the 1960s. The protagonist, Paul, retreats into his own fantasy world, while friends and family come along for the ride. The book is disturbing at times, funny at others, and almost impossible to put down. It was made into a film in 2000, which was wildly popular in Iceland.

Helgason, Hallgrímur. *101 Reykjavík*. 2007. The protagonist, Hlynur, is a lazy, unemployed twentysomething who lives with his mother, watches a lot of pornography, and hangs out in bars in downtown Reykjavík. His life takes a turn when a former girlfriend announces she is pregnant and Hlynur becomes obsessed with his mother's lesbian lover. It's a fun, unexpected tale that was made into a popular movie in Iceland.

Indriðason, Arnaldur. *Jar City.* 2006. Arnaldur is Iceland's leading mystery author. He pens about one book a year, which is great since his tales are so addicting. *Jar City* was the first of Arnaldur's books to feature detective Erlendur Sveinsson, who is a complicated man with a troubled relationship with his family and an obsession with solving Reykjavík's violent crimes. Other characters include his partner, Sigurður Óli, and a female colleague, Elínborg.

Kellogg, Robert. *The Sagas of Icelanders.* 2001. This huge volume includes 10 sagas and 7 shorter tales that give a wonderful overview of Iceland's history and literature. If you're looking for a short introduction, this isn't it. It's comprehensive and glorious.

Laxness, Halldór. *Independent People.* 1946. Laxness remains Iceland's sole recipient of the Nobel Prize for Literature for his novel *Independent People.* The tale follows the life of a Bjartur, a sheep farmer, as he grapples with life, loss, and the sacrifices he made to achieve independence. If you're going to read one Icelandic novel, this should be it.

Internet Resources

Icelandic Tourist Board
www.visiticeland.com
Iceland's tourist board provides a website with pages and pages of information for travelers. The site offers information on festivals, shopping, national parks, and outdoor activities like hiking, bird-watching, whale-watching, and catching the northern lights in the wintertime. There's also information on accommodations, tour operators, and maps.

Iceland Review
www.icelandreview.com
Iceland's main English-language magazine provides features on everything from culture to travel to politics. The website underwent a revamp in 2014 and is worth checking out for in-depth articles as well as columns written by locals.

www.grapevine.is

Reykjavík's go-to English-language newspaper, which is published every two weeks in the summer and monthly in the winter, also maintains a website. You can bone up on local news as well as check out a listings section that details concerts, art exhibitions, and bars.

Visit South Iceland

www.south.is

Covering the south as well as the Reykjanes Peninsula, this tourism site offers detailed information on driving routes, maps, accommodations options, and tour operators. This region encompasses the Golden Circle as well as the Blue Lagoon.

List of Maps

Photo Credits

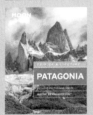

MAP SYMBOLS

Expressway	★	Highlight	✕	Airfield	⚑ Golf Course
Primary Road	○	City/Town	✈	Airport	Ⓟ Parking Area
Secondary Road	⦿	State Capital	▲	Mountain	Archaeological Site
Unpaved Road	⦾	National Capital	✚	Unique Natural Feature	Church
Trail	★	Point of Interest			Gas Station
Ferry	●	Accommodation	⚑	Waterfall	Glacier
Railroad	▼	Restaurant/Bar	⚑	Park	Mangrove
Pedestrian Walkway	■	Other Location	Ⓣ	Trailhead	Reef
Stairs	▲	Campground	✦	Skiing Area	Swamp

CONVERSION TABLES

°C = (°F - 32) / 1.8
°F = (°C x 1.8) + 32
1 inch = 2.54 centimeters (cm)
1 foot = 0.304 meters (m)
1 yard = 0.914 meters
1 mile = 1.6093 kilometers (km)
1 km = 0.6214 miles
1 fathom = 1.8288 m
1 chain = 20.1168 m
1 furlong = 201.168 m
1 acre = 0.4047 hectares
1 sq km = 100 hectares
1 sq mile = 2.59 square km
1 ounce = 28.35 grams
1 pound = 0.4536 kilograms
1 short ton = 0.90718 metric ton
1 short ton = 2,000 pounds
1 long ton = 1.016 metric tons
1 long ton = 2,240 pounds
1 metric ton = 1,000 kilograms
1 quart = 0.94635 liters
1 US gallon = 3.7854 liters
1 Imperial gallon = 4.5459 liters
1 nautical mile = 1.852 km

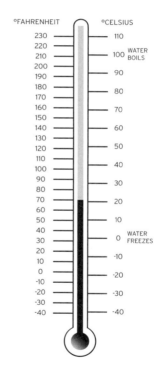

MOON REYKJAVÍK
Avalon Travel
Hachette Book Group
1700 Fourth Street
Berkeley, CA 94710, USA
www.moon.com

Editor: Kristi Mitsuda
Series Manager: Kathryn Ettinger
Copy Editor: Brett Keener
Production and Graphics Coordinator: Darren Alessi
Cover Design: Faceout Studios, Charles Brock
Interior Design: Domini Dragoone
Moon Logo: Tim McGrath
Map Editor: Kat Bennett
Cartographers: Lohnes+Wright, Brian Shotwell, Kat Bennett
Indexer: Greg Jewett

ISBN-13: 9781640496446

Printing History
1st Edition — 2016
2nd Edition — May 2018
5 4 3 2 1